# MᴄLᴀʀᴇɴ

## SPORTS RACING CARS

Dᴀᴠᴇ Fʀɪᴇᴅᴍᴀɴ

**MOTORBOOKS**

First published in 2000 by Motorbooks, an imprint of MBI Publishing Company, Galtier Plaza, Suite 200, 380 Jackson Street, St. Paul, MN 55101-3885 USA

Motorbooks titles are also available at discounts in bulk quantity for industrial or sales-promotional use. For details write to Special Sales Manager at MBI Publishing Company, Galtier Plaza, Suite 200, 380 Jackson Street, St. Paul, MN 55101-3885 USA.

ISBN 0-7603-0724-5

**On the front cover:** For those who were there and for others who simply read about the Canadian-American Challenge Cup races of 1966–1974, orange meant "McLaren," and that meant "champions." During the nine-year history of the series, the McLaren Team won five series titles.

**On the frontispiece:** The "Bruce and Denny Show" was the name thrown at McLaren's domination of Can-Am in 1967. That year, Denny won the first three races. At Laguna Seca, it was going to be Bruce's turn. McLaren took the checkered flag to win his first of many Can-Am races.

**On the title page:** The powerful McLaren team, Bruce McLaren (4) and Denny Hulme (5), drew a crowd wherever it went in 1967. This one gathers as the team prepares to qualify at Riverside.

**On the back cover:** Top: The last race for Bruce McLaren's Cooper-Oldsmobile in 1964 was the Tourist Trophy at Goodwill. McLaren (2) sits on the pole, having broken Hugh Dibley's track record by no less than three seconds. Jim Clark's (1) Lotus 30 is barely seen at the far right while Denis Hulme's (8) Brabham BT8, Hugh P. K. Dibley's (7) Brabham BT8, and David Piper's (4) Ferrari 250LM are in the background. McLaren led the race from the beginning, only to retire disappointingly with clutch problems.

**Bottom:** The McLaren M8B was a dominant weapon in 1969. Here, the M8Bs of McLaren (4) and Hulme (5) line up on the front row at Edmonton to begin the fourth round of the Can-Am series. The McLaren team not only won this race, but every other round in the 11-race series that year.

**End papers:** It seems that everyone was sprouting wings by the time the Can-Am series reached Bridgehampton in 1969. As usual, Denny Hulme (5) and Bruce McLaren (4) in their M8Bs, led from the start and finished first and second. There was never another season in Can-Am so dominated by a pair of drivers as the "Bruce and Denny Show."

Edited by John Adams-Graf
Designed by Tom Heffron

Printed in Hong Kong

# CONTENTS

# PREFACE

"Most of the people who work here have no idea who Bruce McLaren was nor do they have any idea that if it weren't for the original sports cars that we built, McLaren International and McLaren Cars Ltd. would not exist today." This shocking comment came from Gordon Murray, in 1991, during one of my early visits to his office in Woking, Surrey, Great Britain. Those comments set me thinking: How was this possible? Doesn't anyone who works for a company with a legendary past care enough to investigate the company's history? I guess the answer to that question is pretty simple.

When McLaren quit the Can-Am series at the end of the 1972 season, the company's concentration turned to single-seat racing. Over the years, a succession of highly successful F1, F5000, and Indy Car programs have pushed the memory of the sports car–building company further from the minds of those who replaced many of the original employees. With the exception of the excellent books done by Eion Young and Doug Nye, no other author has covered any other aspect of McLaren's racing history other than F1 in depth. There have been numerous books about McLaren published in the past several years, and they all say exactly the same thing —they all talk about Formula 1 and forget about the sports car racing roots of the company. This is why I wrote this book.

To my knowledge, no other book has covered just McLaren sports racing cars. The time has come to remind racing fans around the world that the McLaren team they see racing today was built on the reputation and money earned from sports car racing in the past.

—Dave Friedman
Newport Beach, California

# ACKNOWLEDGMENTS

This book has been a long time coming, and it was the people at MBI Publishing Company who finally saw the potential for it. Tim Parker, Zack Miller, and John Adams-Graf are responsible for helping me get this done. Gordon Murray of McLaren Cars Ltd. provided a considerable amount of material, support, and encouragement over the years, and Richard Ward of The Team in London also provided valuable assistance. Dan Gurney, Chris Amon, Bob Bondurant, John Cannon, Lothar Motschenbacher, Sam Posey, and Augie Pabst contributed to the interviews. Kathy Ager at LAT Photographic assisted me with supplemental photographs. Susan Claudius read and corrected much of the manuscript and captions for this book, and she provided the female understanding so necessary to complete one of these projects.

To all of the above individuals, a huge thank you. It couldn't have been done without you.

# CHAPTER 1

# EARLY McLAREN

## 1958-1963

**W**ho knew that when Bruce McLaren started racing in his native homeland of New Zealand in the early 1950s that within a very few years he would be the guiding light behind a company that would grow to legendary proportions?

McLaren started his racing in a 1929 Ulster Austin Seven that he and his father bought. This Austin Seven became the foundation for what was to come later. Bruce progressed from the Austin to an Austin Healey 100, a bob-tailed Cooper sports car, and then to a 1,750-cc Cooper in which he won the "Driver to Europe" award in 1958.

Signing with the Cooper team for 1959, McLaren became the teammate of Jack Brabham. By the end of this first season with Cooper, Bruce became the youngest driver (22) ever to win a Grand Prix. He won the first U.S. Grand Prix at Sebring in December 1959. The 1960 season brought an early win at the Argentine Grand Prix and a second place in the final points standings. Between 1960 and 1963, McLaren also successfully campaigned Cooper Monacos, Aston Martins, Austin Healey Sprites, Sunbeam Alpines, and various other sports and GT cars.

At the end of 1963, McLaren formed his own team. By 1964, he began to build and campaign his own sports cars. Even though the Cooper F1 program had been on a downhill slide since the beginning of 1961, McLaren stayed with Cooper through the end of 1964 when he finally left to build his own F1 car.

Bruce McLaren emerged as a brilliant driver, designer, car builder, and engineer. In addition to his own program, Bruce also became involved with the Ford Le Mans program from the very beginning. His contributions to the Ford Team were unequaled by anyone else, except for Ken Miles. McLaren's work with Ford was rewarded when he and Chris Amon won the 1966 Le Mans 24 Hour Race driving a Shelby American–entered Ford Mk.II. This noteworthy win was the first of Ford's four consecutive Le Mans wins.

Bruce McLaren works on his first racing car, an Austin Seven Ulster, in Auckland, New Zealand. McLaren and his dad bought this car in 1952. Bruce raced it until 1955, when he sold it to buy an Austin Healey 100.

In 1958, Bruce McLaren won the New Zealand "Driver to Europe" award. His outstanding performances in a Cooper F2 landed him an F1 contract with the Cooper team in 1959. The first United States Grand Prix was run at Sebring in December 1959. Bruce McLaren's Cooper 45 (9) can be seen at the far left of this starting picture. Also visible are Bob Said (18), Connaught; Harry Schell (19), Cooper 51; Phil Hill (5), Ferrari Dino 246; Alan Stacey (11), Lotus 16; Maurice Trintignant (6), Cooper 51; Jack Brabham (8), Cooper 51; Stirling Moss (7), Cooper 51; Tony Brooks (2), Ferrari Dino 246; Cliff Allison (3), Ferrari Dino 246; Wolfgang von Trips (4), Ferrari Dino 246; Innes Ireland (10), Lotus 16; and Roy Salvadori (12), Cooper 45.

Bruce McLaren won his first Grand Prix at Sebring in 1959 and, at the age of 22, became the youngest driver ever to win a Grand Prix. McLaren finished sixth in the final standings, while his teammate, Jack Brabham, won the World Championship and Cooper won the Constructor's Championship.

In October 1960, Bruce McLaren made his first appearance in the professional road races that were being held during that time in California. At the Pacific Grand Prix at Laguna Seca, McLaren drove the Cunningham E-Type Jaguar Prototype that Jack Brabham had driven the previous weekend at Riverside. Longtime Cunningham chief mechanic Alfred Momo (right), Jack Flaherty (center, wearing a driver's suit), and Bruce McLaren (rear, in the dark sweater) push the Jaguar to the starting grid. McLaren finished 14th overall, but better days would soon come in those professional races.

McLaren's 1960 Grand Prix season was highlighted by a win at Argentina and three second-place finishes. Once again, Brabham won the World Championship, but this time McLaren finished second in the year-end standings. Cooper also won the Constructors Championship for the second year in a row. After the completion of the 1960 season, and the finish of 2.5-liter formula for F1 cars, Cooper's domination of Grand Prix racing fell by the wayside and was never regained.

At the March 1961, Sebring 4-Hour Race for GT cars under 1,000 cc, Bruce McLaren drove a right-hand-drive Austin Sprite to fourth overall.

Bruce McLaren, partnered with Walt Hansgen in the white-and-blue-striped Cunningham Maserati Tipo 63, retired in the fourth hour of the 1961 Sebring 12-Hour Race with rear axle problems.

In the closest and most exciting race seen at Riverside's Los Angeles Times Grand Prix up until that time, Bruce McLaren's (6) Cooper Monaco and Jack Brabham's (4) Cooper Monaco gave the 1961 record-breaking crowd of 70,600 something to really cheer about. Racing wheel-to-wheel and exchanging the lead on almost every lap, McLaren and Brabham finished one-two, but Brabham took the win.

Cooper teammates Jack Brabham and Bruce McLaren share a light moment prior to the start of practice at Laguna Seca in October 1961.

A wonderful starting field that included Stirling Moss (1), Lotus 19; Bruce McLaren (6), Cooper Monaco; Roger Penske (16), Cooper Monaco; Dan Gurney (96), Lotus 19; Peter Ryan (83), Lotus 19; Jim Hall (66), Chaparral 1; and Jack Brabham (4), Cooper Monaco. Here they leave the start-finish line for the first heat of the October 1961 Pacific Grand Prix at Laguna Seca.

Bruce McLaren (6), Cooper Monaco, and Dan Gurney (96), Lotus 19, are in close competition at Laguna Seca. McLaren finished third overall behind Moss (winner) and Brabham, who finished second.

After winning the 1962 Sebring 3-Hour Race for under 1,000-cc GT cars, Bruce McLaren (right) accepts the winner's trophy and the congratulations of second-place finisher Walt Hansgen (left). Alfred Momo stands between Hansgen and McLaren. Both McLaren and Hansgen drove Cunningham Team 1,000-cc Fiat Abarths.

Alfred Momo stands at the front of the cockpit of the Cunningham Cooper-Maserati, while driver Bruce McLaren checks his eyesight and co-driver Roger Penske checks the rear decklid. This car was one of the two Cunningham Team entries for the March 1962 Sebring 12-Hour Race.

Bruce McLaren (shown) and Roger Penske drove this Cooper-Maserati to fifth place overall at Sebring in 1962.

A 3-Hour Endurance Race was staged as a prelude to the October 1962 *Times* Grand Prix at Riverside. Bruce McLaren (pictured here) and Jack Brabham drove a pair of Sunbeam Alpines in that race, but mechanical woes put them both permanently into the pits before the race ended.

John Cooper (left) and Bruce McLaren engage in a last-minute discussion prior to the start of the main event at the October 1962 Times Grand Prix.

By 1962, the *Times* Grand Prix had turned into one of the premier sports car races in the world. This race annually drew record crowds to Riverside to watch a virtual who's-who of the world's top racing talent. Bruce McLaren (5), Cooper Monaco, passes Lloyd Ruby (26), Lotus 19, in the Riverside esses on his way to a fourth overall finish.

The Pacific Grand Prix at Laguna Seca, run a week after the *Times* Grand Prix at Riverside, also drew a large, international field of drivers and teams. Always hoping to capitalize on the name drivers who came over for Riverside, Laguna Seca had a policy for paying little starting money. That policy cost them a number of top entries for their race. In October 1962, Roger Penske's (6) Cooper-Zerex Special and Walt Hansgen's (63) Cooper-Buick lead the all-star starting field on their way to Turn 1. Following Penske and Hansgen are Lloyd Ruby (26), Lotus 19; Dan Gurney (96), Lotus 19; Bruce McLaren (5), Cooper Monaco; Jim Hall (66), Chaparral 1; Masten Gregory (3), Lotus 19; Graham Hill (55), Cooper Monaco; Innes Ireland (15), Lotus 19; Tim Mayer (17), Cooper Monaco; Alan Connell (55), Cooper Monaco; and a pack of others.

Battling for position on Laguna Seca's famed corkscrew in the 1962 Pacific Grand Prix are Bruce McLaren's (5) Cooper Monaco, Masten Gregory's (3) Lotus 19, and Walt Hansgen's (63) Cooper-Buick.

In spite of a wild spin down the corkscrew, McLaren regained control to finish third overall in the 1962 Pacific Grand Prix.

During 1963, Bruce McLaren drove one of the beautiful factory-backed Aston Martin 214s in selected endurance races. In June McLaren drove the Aston with Innes Ireland at Le Mans, but the engine blew up in the fifth hour, putting them out of the race. At the Tourist Trophy in August 1963, both Astons, driven by Ireland and McLaren, were hampered by homologation problems regarding the width of their wheels. These wheel problems also caused some serious handling problems, spinning the Astons numerous times during the race. Engine problems also caused McLaren to pit several times before finally retiring from the race. Driving furiously, Innes Ireland finally finished, placing fourth overall. Ireland would have won the Tourist Trophy easily if the cars were equipped with the proper wheels.

# CHARTING
# A COURSE

By the end of 1963, it was not a question of whether McLaren was going to race, but rather, how and when the company was going to race. This dilemma was created by a difference of opinion among the company members about what approach to take.

For the 1964 season, Bruce McLaren wanted to build a lightweight, Climax-powered car that would be based loosely on the Zerex Special that Roger Penske raced so successfully for the previous two seasons. On the other hand, McLaren's mechanics, Tyler Alexander and Wally Wilmott, strongly felt that the Climax-powered cars were a thing of the past. The two had been to Nassau the previous December and had seen firsthand how competitive the American engine sports cars were. After watching the American cars soundly thrash the European opposition, Alexander and Wilmott believed that they should follow the North American approach. This was sound thinking because the biggest and most lucrative races on their calendar would be held in North America.

Until a McLaren-built sports racing car could be completed, a stop-gap measure was needed. Bruce McLaren found it with the ex-Penske Zerex Special that John Mecom's racing team had deemed expendable. The Zerex, shouldering a 2.7-liter Climax engine, had been parked after the disastrous 1963 Nassau race. There was some discussion on the Mecom team about converting the Zerex to American power using an aluminum 3.5-liter Oldsmobile F85, but the Mecom crew never found the time to do so. When Teddy Mayer approached John Mecom about buying the car complete with the Climax and the Oldsmobile engines, Mecom agreed to sell. Mecom Racing rushed the Zerex off to England in order for Mayer's people to prepare it for a race at Oulton Park several days later. To do so, several additions had to be made to the car to conform to the complex English scrutinizing laws. Among the necessary changes were the addition of a luggage trunk, headlights, and a windshield wiper.

The Zerex Special debuted at the *Los Angeles Times* Grand Prix at Riverside in October 1962. This picture demonstrates the deluxe passenger seating accommodations for any interested takers. A startled Bruce McLaren checks the Zerex out from the car in the background.

The McLaren team raced the Zerex, or as they called it, the "Cooper-Oldsmobile," with great success. Of the six races entered between April and August 1964, the McLaren team recorded four wins and two DNFs. By August, the new ground-up, McLaren-built M1A was ready for testing and the car made its racing debut at the Canadian Sports Car Grand Prix at Mosport, Canada, in September. Also running at Riverside, Laguna Seca, and Nassau, the M1A was always among the fastest cars, but it didn't win any of these events. Nagging problems undid the cars, but in spite of the setbacks, the McLaren legacy was born.

For 1965, Chris Amon was signed as the second McLaren driver, and a new car, the M1B with a body designed by famed motor sport artist Michael Turner, was conceived. The 1965 M1B was designed to accept the Chevrolet, Oldsmobile, and Ford engines. Nevertheless, McLaren's choice of engines was still the lighter, Traco-built, aluminum Oldsmobile. The team was willing to give away a lot of power to save the difference in weight. The M1B proved to be extremely competitive, although the McLaren drivers had their hands full trying to contend with the Chevrolet-powered Chaparral 2 and the 6-liter, Chevrolet-powered Lola T70. By the end of the season, it was obvious that there was no substitute for cubic inches. Team McLaren finally scored its first real successes with the M1B, and the world had a sample of what was to come.

The first car to be run by Bruce McLaren under the McLaren team banner had a highly successful and controversial history prior to the time that McLaren took delivery of it. The Zerex Special was built by Roy Gane in his Pennsylvania Updraft Engineering shop for a young racing driver named Roger Penske. Gane took the wrecked ex-Cunningham Formula One Cooper and turned it into a center-seat sports car after the SCCA technical inspectors approved the car's novel design concept. Note how far to the left the seat sits in the frame. The rules clearly stated that a passenger seat must be placed in the chassis. A 2.7-liter Climax engine rests in the chassis.

Roy Gane prepares the 2.7 Climax engine for installation in the Zerex Special. The engine was Jack Brabham's spare during his 1961 Indianapolis effort with the Cooper Cars' team before Ganes acquired it for the Zerex Special.

The Zerex's debut race at Riverside resulted in a victory over a world-class field of cars and drivers. A week later, at Laguna Seca, Penske won again, making a clean sweep of the world's two richest sports car races. Although the car met the letter of the law, it didn't really meet the spirit of the law and that was where all of the protests originated. Actor Dick Van Dyke (right, in coat and tie) checks out the car.

By late 1962, the Zerex Special was banned from any further racing activity until modifications to the chassis's configuration could be made, conforming it to regulations. By the start of the 1963 season, Gane had widened the chassis and moved the steering from the center of the car. Although no competitor, and few officials, thought it was still legal, the car was allowed to race, but it never again achieved the success that it had in 1962.

After the beginning of the 1963 season, Penske made a package deal with John Mecom that transferred his team consisting of himself, the Cooper-Zerex Special, and Roy Gane to the Mecom Racing Team. The high point of the 1963 season for Penske and the Zerex was a brilliant victory in the August Guards Trophy Race at Brands Hatch.

By the end of 1963, the Zerex's power-to-weight advantage was stripped away by the V-8 power of the new rear-engine Chaparral and the Shelby American King Cobras. In spite of the disadvantage in horsepower, Penske still managed to finish second overall at the *Times* Grand Prix in October against a large international field of drivers and top flight equipment. The old girl still had some staying power.

Bruce McLaren bought the Zerex in April 1964 and rushed it to England to compete at Oulton Park, but the car retired because of no oil pressure. A week later at the Aintree 200, McLaren was more successful with the Climax-powered Zerex. He won the race by beating Jim Clark, who was driving his first race in a Ford-powered Lotus 30. Here, Bruce McLaren leads Peter Arundell's Lotus 23 during the Aintree 200.

The final race for the Climax-powered Zerex was the Daily Express International Trophy Race at Silverstone in May 1964. McLaren, once again, came up a winner, beating Roy Salvadori in a potent Cooper Maserati. Note the addition of windshield wipers, headlights, and redesigned fenders to accommodate the wider tires on the Zerex. These modifications were all necessary for the inclement conditions encountered while racing in England.

The newly completed Cooper-Oldsmobile sits in the overcrowded workshop in New Malden before shipment to Mosport. This photograph shows the newly replaced frame and the installation of the Oldsmobile V-8.

The first outing for the newly modified Cooper Oldsmobile was the June 1964 Player's 200 at Mosport, Canada. Jim Clark (back to camera) keeps Tyler Alexander (far left), Bruce McLaren, Dan Gurney, Ken Miles, and Wally Wilmott entertained during a practice break.

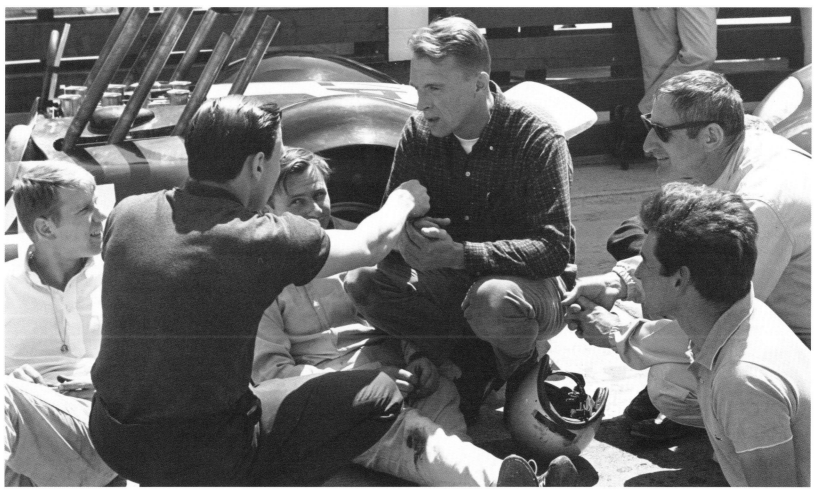

Jim Clark (left) and Bruce McLaren share a light moment before the start of the race. Clark, who was scheduled to drive a V-8-powered Lotus 19, opted not to because, in his opinion, the car was "a load of rubbish." Rather than drive a car he deemed "dangerous and undriveable," Clark chose to participate as a spectator.

The much-modified Cooper-Oldsmobile sits on the starting grid at Mosport in June 1964. The entire center section of the chassis was scrapped and replaced by a McLaren-built tube frame to accommodate the Traco-built, 4.0-liter, aluminum, Oldsmobile engine. Note the pipe organ exhaust system that had to be used because the team's preparation time ran out before a proper exhaust system could be fabricated. Teddy Mayer (left) and Wally Wilmott tend to the McLaren entry, while Roger Penske (6) in his Chaparral 2 seems ready for the starter's flag.

This rare color shot of the McLaren Cooper-Oldsmobile at Mosport shows the car's dark green paint with a silver stripe, which sparked the nickname Jolly Green Giant.

McLaren's (47) Cooper-Oldsmobile tries to dive under A. J. Foyt's (8) Scarab as they both dip under Allen Grant's (181) Cheetah.

Bruce McLaren leads Jim Hall's (66) Chaparral 2 and A. J. Foyt's (8) Scarab during one of the heats of the Player's 200. McLaren posted the second fastest qualifying time and won both heats of the Mosport race. Not too bad for a two-year-old racing car.

Bruce McLaren and Tyler Alexander take a victory lap at Mosport. This was the first major win for the McLaren team.

When the Cooper-Oldsmobile showed up for the Guards Trophy Race at Brands Hatch in August, the car was sporting repaired bodywork, a brand new paint job, and a proper exhaust system. During practice and qualifying, McLaren broke the track record several times.

Bruce McLaren ran away with the Guard's Trophy Race in spite of heavy international competition who were favorites to win. The new McLaren chassis really improved the handling of the car, and coupled with the 4.0-liter Traco engine, it made for an unbeatable combination.

The last race for the Cooper-Oldsmobile was the Goodwood Tourist Trophy in August 1964. Bruce McLaren (2) sits on the pole, having broken Hugh Dibley's track record by no less than three seconds. Jim Clark's (1) Lotus 30 is barely seen at the far right while Denis Hulme's (8) Brabham BT8, Hugh P. K. Dibley's (7) Brabham BT8, and David Piper's (4) Ferrari 275LM are in the background. McLaren led the race from the beginning only to disappointingly retire with clutch problems.

At the same time that Bruce McLaren was winning the Guards Trophy and competing in the Tourist Trophy, work on the first real McLaren sports car was being completed. The car, designated the M1A, was to make its race debut at Mosport in September and go on to compete in the West Coast Pro Series at Riverside and Laguna Seca. The M1A's season concluded at Nassau in December. Bruce McLaren (left) Wally Willmott, Bruce Harre, Howden Ganley, and Eoin Young study the scale model of the first all-McLaren-built sports car.

The first space frame McLaren sports car was built in the 4,000-square-foot shop at Feltham. The frame for the M1A sits on work stands in the foreground. The Cooper-Oldsmobile and a Tasman Series Cooper undergo preparation in the background.

Bruce McLaren conducts a body-off test at Goodwood during the summer of 1964.

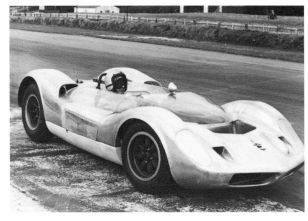

The first McLaren M1A sports car is being tested at Goodwood in early September 1964. This first test with the full body mounted on the car resulted in McLaren besting his own track record by three seconds. The "Strong Mother" printed on the side of the door panel referred to the Traco-built, 4.0-liter, aluminum Oldsmobile engine. One of the new Bruce McLaren Motor Racing Team stickers, designed by artist Michael Turner, appears on the nose of the car.

The beautifully prepared McLaren M1A drew a lot of spectators upon its arrival at Mosport in September 1964.

The low-slung M1A sits in the pits prior to going out for practice at Mosport. "Strong Mother," the name first applied on the prototype in England, was retained, now appearing under the exhaust pipes.

This picture accentuates the superb craftsmanship and attention to detail that became a McLaren trademark. Bruce McLaren receives a push start from Wally Willmott, Teddy Mayer, and Tyler Alexander.

When the green flag fell, McLaren took an immediate lead from Jim Hall's (66) Chaparral 2, George Wintersteen's (12) Cooper-Chevrolet, and Ludivico Scarfiotti's (3) Ferrari 330P. McLaren's 1.30.6 qualifying time was second fastest only to Hall's Chaparral 2, which qualified at 1.29.5. The difference between the fastest and slowest qualifier at Mosport was an astounding 29 seconds, a very dangerous situation at best.

McLaren led the first 55 laps after his closest competition, Jim Hall, was involved in a spectacular crash on the first lap. On lap 56, a broken throttle linkage forced McLaren into the pits. By the time repairs were completed, he had dropped to seventh place.

After returning to the race, McLaren tied the old lap record four times and broke it seven times in his charge to the front. Unfortunately, time ran out, and McLaren finished in third place, three laps down to the winner, Pedro Rodriguez.

The wonderfully fitted exhaust system on the M1A is clearly visible in this photograph taken at Riverside. It was a far cry from the one seen on the Cooper-Oldsmobile at Mosport just four months earlier. Also note the aluminum, 4-liter, F85 Oldsmobile engine fitted with the Hewland gearbox.

Bruce McLaren seems to be smiling as he sets the second-fastest qualifying time at Riverside. Note the quickly hand-painted number on the side of the M1A.

The start of the 20-lap qualifying race for the over 2-liter cars presents the typical all-star line-up that was commonplace during the *L.A. Times* Grand Prix in the 1960s. Heading for Riverside's very fast Turn 1 are Parnelli Jones (94) King Cobra, Bruce McLaren's (2) McLaren M1A, Dan Gurney's (19) Lotus 19-Ford, Jim Clark's (15) Lotus 30, Jerry Grant's (8) Lotus 19-Chevy, Bob Bondurant's (93) King Cobra, Walt Hansgen's (26) Scarab, Hap Sharp's (66) Chaparral 2, Augie Pabst's (25) Genie-Chevy, Bobby Unser's (96) Lotus 19-Chevy, Roger Penske's (6) Chaparral 2, Ronnie Bucknum's (95) King Cobra, and Richie Ginther's (92) King Cobra. A. J. Foyt's (23) Hussein and Ken Miles' (98) Cobra 289 lurk in the middle of the field.

A spectacular race between the two fastest qualifiers (Bruce McLaren's (2) McLaren M1A and Dan Gurney's (19) Lotus 19-Ford) developed in the 20-lap over 2-liter qualifying race. After numerous lead changes, Gurney fell out and McLaren won the race by 29 seconds.

Starting from the pole, McLaren (2) leads A. J. Foyt's (23) Hussein 1, Parnelli Jones' (94) Shelby American King Cobra, and Walt Hansgen's (26) Scarab into Riverside's famed Turn 7. While nine seconds in the lead, McLaren's water hose blew off, and he had to pit for repairs. After spending four minutes in the pits, McLaren fought his way back to third place only to have the hose pop off again, forcing him to retire from the race.

The McLaren M1A undergoes its race preparation in a garage in downtown Monterey before the start of practice at Laguna Seca.

Bruce McLaren's (47) McLaren M1A leads Trevor Taylor's (18) Brabham BT8 out of Laguna Seca's Turn 9 during the October 1964 Monterey Grand Prix. McLaren qualified fourth, but, once again, water hose problems caused an early retirement for the car.

During the six weeks between the end of the race at Laguna Seca and the start of the Nassau Speed Weeks in December, the car received a fresh new look. Wally Willmott pushes the newly painted *red* McLaren M1A off of the old military LST (landing ship tank) that transported some of the cars from Florida to Nassau.

Bruce McLaren downs the bubbly after winning the Formula Vee race in Nassau. In the background, Eion Young awaits his turn at the champagne.

Bruce McLaren had to catch a nap wherever he could between Nassau practice sessions.

The new McLaren colors of red and silver were seen by many as an improvement over the previous color scheme. The new color, though, didn't improve the performance—the car only lasted five laps in the Nassau Governor's Trophy Race.

During the Nassau Trophy Race, Bruce McLaren's (5) McLaren M1A leads Newton Davis' (33) Lotus 30, Don Sesslar's (74) Sunbeam Tiger, George Garrett's (71) Bobsy Ford, and Tom Payne's (73) Shelby Cobra through the esses curves.

Bruce McLaren makes the required pit stop during the Nassau Trophy Race. McLaren finished second overall.

Bruce and Patty McLaren reap the harvest during the awards dinner at the conclusion of the Nassau Speed Weeks.

One of the most anticipated and popular displays at the London Racing Car Show in January 1965 was the premiere showing of the McLaren-Elva-Oldsmobile. In November 1964, McLaren signed a deal with Elva Cars Ltd. to produce the M1A as a customer car. Since Elva cars was set up as a production facility, the deal allowed the McLaren factory to concentrate on racing and building prototypes. Eventually, 24 of the customer M1As, known as the Elva-McLaren Mk1s, were built.

It's early 1965 and Bruce McLaren is testing his M1A. Could this be the car with the Ferguson two-speed automatic transmission?

Bruce McLaren was involved in the Ford GT program from its inception in early 1964, but it wasn't until the program was transferred to Shelby American that he was able to achieve any measure of success from his long hours of labor. At Sebring in March 1965, McLaren and co-driver Ken Miles (11) finished second overall to the Hall/Sharp (3) Chaparral 2 and won the prototype class. Among the other competitors in this picture are Bruce Jennings (4), Chaparral 2; Pedro Rodriguez (30), Ferrari 330P; Dan Gurney (23), Lotus 19-Ford; David Piper (31), Ferrari 250LM; Bob Johnson (14), Daytona Cobra Coupe; Bob Grossman (26), Ferrari 330P; Mark Donohue (29), Ferrari 250LM; and Ed Leslie (12), Daytona Cobra Coupe.

Bruce McLaren finished second to Jim Clark at the International Trophy Race at Goodwood in April 1965. McLaren won the May Daily Express International Trophy at Silverstone, and Chris Amon won the July Martini International Trophy at Silverstone in this M1A. By mid-1965, it had become apparent to the McLaren team that the F85 Oldsmobile engine wasn't producing the horsepower that was necessary to compete regularly with the Ford and Chevrolet engines in the Lola T70s and the Lotus 30s.

The Tourist Trophy run at Oulton Park in April 1965 was the only time in which the McLaren team would ever use an automatic transmission in competition. McLaren (9) leads Jim Clark's (4) Lotus 30 and Frank Gardiner's (23) Willment Cobra Coupe early in the first heat. A transmission leak forced the M1A out while leading the first heat, and a blown engine parked the car while running second in Heat 2. After this race, the team realized that the cost of developing the automatic transmission would be prohibitive and the project was put aside.

John Coundley (11) was one of the earliest buyers of a Mark 1 Elva-McLaren-Oldsmobile. Coundley leads David Hobbs' (2) Lola T70 during the Oulton Park Tourist Trophy. Coundley finished 15th overall, while Hobbs finished in a very disputed 2nd place.

Start of the June 1965 Player's 200 has Jim Hall's (66) Chaparral 2, Walt McKay's (93) Cooper-Ford, and Hugh P. K. Dibley's (5) Lola T70 leading an impressive field off of the starting line. McLaren lurks in the back of the field.

Bruce McLaren led both heats of the Player's 200 but was put out, first, by brake problems and then by a broken gearbox. Here, McLaren (4) leads Joe Buzzetta's (3) Elva-Porsche at Moss Corner. The McLaren team was now using a 5-liter, Traco F85 Oldsmobile engine.

At the August 1965 Brands Hatch Guards Trophy, Peter Revson's (38) Brabham BT8 is lapped by Bruce McLaren (7) who was on his way to a second-place finish behind John Surtees' Lola T70. The 5-liter Oldsmobile engine was completely outclassed by the 6-liter Chevrolet engine powering Surtees' car.

John Coundley's (22) Elva-McLaren leads David Hobbs (1) Lola T70 and Jackie Stewart's (5) Lola T70 during the Guards Trophy race. Coundley finished eighth overall, Stewart finished third overall, and Hobbs failed to finish.

Graham Hill's (21) Elva McLaren passes Jim Clark's parked Lotus 40 as he exits the pits during the Guards Trophy. Hill retired with mechanical problems. The John Coombs team McLaren Mark 1 was the first customer car to be delivered by Elva Cars Ltd.

A body-off look at the McLaren M1A reveals the tubular frame, independent suspension, 5-liter, aluminum F85 Oldsmobile engine, and German-manufactured ZF four-speed transmission. This particular car finished second at the Guards Trophy in August 1965.

*I admired Bruce and his operation as highly professional and extremely competitive. We were great friends off of the track, and we shared many good times. On the track, Bruce was a very tough and fair competitor, and we had some very memorable races together.*— JIM HALL

Bruce McLaren and Jim Hall (background) admired each other immensely, and although they were tough competitors on the track, they were great friends off of it. McLaren once remarked that when he came up with a new idea, he usually found out that Hall had already tried it on his Chaparrals months before.

Bruce McLaren seems to be wondering if it's time to go out and practice for the September 1965 Canadian Sports Car Grand Prix at Mosport.

The McLaren team unveiled the lightweight 427-ci-powered Ford X1 roadster at Mosport. Developed for Ford, the team hoped that this project would enable Ford to build a competitive Group 7 car out of the existing GT40 roadster. Unfortunately, that was not to be. Chris Amon was given the unfortunate task of driving the car, dubbed Big Ed, after Ford's less-than-successful Edsel project. According to Amon, "That car was absolutely terrible. It was far too heavy, and it was grossly underpowered. There was no way that I could compete with the McLarens, Lolas, and Chaparrals that I had to race against. In my opinion, the whole project was a waste of time. I believe that the only reason Bruce took on that job was because Ford paid him a rather substantial retainer."

Bruce McLaren debuted the new Michael Turner–bodied McLaren M1B at Mosport in September 1965. This new car had a new, lighter chassis that was similar to the M1A. The Oldsmobile engine was still retained for the remainder of the 1965 season, but provisions were in place to accommodate either a Ford or Chevrolet engine at a later time. This car was marketed in the United States as the Elva-McLaren Mark 2. Twenty-eight Mark 2s were eventually built. Here, McLaren leads Bud Gates' (73) McLaren M1A through Moss Corner during the Canadian Grand Prix for Sports Cars.

Bruce McLaren's (14) McLaren M1B and Jim Hall's (66) Chaparral 2 had a tremendous battle for the lead in both heats of the Mosport race. McLaren won the first heat, and Hall won the second heat by just a few feet. David Piper's (25) Ferrari P2 trails Hall.

Augie Pabst's brand new McLaren M1A caught fire and was totally destroyed early in the September 1965 Mosport race. Fortunately, Pabst was not hurt in the spectacular blaze that completely consumed his car.

Bruce McLaren (left) and Jim Hall (right) share the winner's rostrum at Mosport. Hall was declared the overall winner of the race, with McLaren in second by a very slight margin.

Phil Hill substituted for Bruce McLaren at the September 1965 Northwest Grand Prix at Kent, Washington. Hill finished second to Jim Hall in the first heat, and in the second a sticking throttle forced Hill to lose a lap in the pits in the second. Phil finished 11th overall in the final standings.

The Monterey Grand Prix at Laguna Seca was next on the schedule but the McLaren team, and the other European teams, passed on that event because of a dispute over starting money. The crown jewel of the North American Professional Racing Series was the *Los Angeles Times* Grand Prix at Riverside held at the end of October. By that race, the M1B was equipped with bigger brakes and wider front tires. McLaren led the race by a large margin until one of his tires began to go flat and he had to pit to change it. As McLaren approaches Turn 7, note the front lip spoiler and the cockpit cooling duct added specifically for this race.

Chris Amon drove the Ford X1 to fifth overall at the *Times* Grand Prix. A rear spoiler and a front spoiler had been added to the bodywork since the Mosport race in September.

Bruce McLaren laps the Ford X1 between Riverside's Turn 6 and 7 as Chris Amon looks on. McLaren went on to finish third overall while Amon finished fifth overall.

Bruce McLaren's (47) McLaren M1B led the Nassau Governor's Trophy race from the second lap until the conclusion. Behind McLaren are Jim Hall's (66) Chaparral 2C, Hap Sharp's (65) Chaparral 2, and Bob Bondurant's (111) Lola T70.

Chris Amon's (4) Ford X1 also competed in the Governor's Trophy race but ran into mechanical trouble and finished 17th overall in spite of not even finishing the race. Art Ackerley's (48) MGB trails Amon. The McLaren team tried an automatic transmission in the X1 during practice but decided to run the regular manual gearbox in the race. After the Nassau Speedweeks concluded, this car returned to Kar Kraft in Dearborn and then was sent to Shelby American for modification as an endurance car. Ken Miles and Lloyd Ruby drove it to victory at Sebring in March 1966. After Sebring, the car returned to Shelby American where it was cut up. Today, it resides in some landfill under a Los Angeles apartment complex.

Bruce McLaren (foreground), Bob Bondurant, Jim Hall, and Charlie Hayes relax prior to the Le Mans start of the Nassau Trophy Race. McLaren did not finish the race due to engine problems.

# CHAPTER 3

# BUILDING A WINNER

The year 1966 was marked with many changes in the way Group 7 cars were campaigned. First of all, the Royal Auto Club (RAC) bowed to the pressure applied by the British oil companies, ruling that 1966 would be the last season that the crowd-pleasing "Big Bangers" would compete in Britain. This poorly calculated—and obviously political—decision created a huge outcry from the press, fans, and drivers, but it was to no avail. Although the Group 7 races vastly outdrew the single-seat F1 and F2 events, there was absolutely no reconsideration of the ruling.

In February, it was formally announced that the Canadian-American (Can-Am) Challenge Cup series would hold its first race in September 1966. By the end of the year, six Can-Am races were held: two (St. Jovite and Mosport) in Canada and four (Bridgehampton, Laguna Seca, Riverside, and Las Vegas) in the United States. The USRRC also ran eight races prior to the first Can-Am event. This series provided the North American drivers and teams with an opportunity to prepare to meet the world's best in the upcoming fall series.

The McLaren team relied on an updated version of the tried-and-true M1B for this first Can-Am season. This revised M1B incorporated a stiffer frame, wider rear body pane to allow for wider wheels, and, in the Can-Am version, a 330-cid Chevrolet engine. The team cars started off with four-speed Hewland gearboxes, but switched to German-built ZF gearboxes in an effort to help reduce the car's overall weight. The M1Bs proved to be very competitive, but they were never quite good enough to beat the Lolas and Chaparrals. Several upgrades were made to the team cars toward the end of the Can-Am season. McLaren fitted larger, fuel-injected 364-cid Chevrolet engines in both cars for the last three races. The team was fitted a movable rear spoiler on McLaren's car at Riverside and Las Vegas. In spite of these changes, the car was not a winner.

Bud Morley (6) and Lothar Motschenbacher (27) run their McLaren Mk. 2s in tandem early in the May 1966 USRRC race at Riverside. Neither driver finished the race, but Motschenbacher came from well back in the field to lead the race before blowing his engine eight laps from the finish. The production version of the McLaren M1B was referred to as the Elva McLaren Mk. 2. Twenty-eight of the M1B, Mk. 2 McLarens were built.

As was originally hoped, the USRRC series provided a large market for the Elva-McLaren Mk. 2. Twenty-eight of the M1B/Mk. 2 models were built and run with moderate success by a number of independent teams. Charlie Hayes won at Laguna Seca, Lothar Motschenbacher won at Mid-Ohio, and Chuck Parsons won the Road America 500 and the USRRC championship. It would be unfair, however, to say that Parsons won the championship in a McLaren car. Parsons drove several different cars during the series, but his only win of the year did occur in a McLaren Mk. 2.

The McLaren team was not satisfied with second place, and in 1967, mounted a renewed Can-Am effort. In the spring of 1967, six months prior to the first race, Robin Herd and Gordon Coppuck completed designs on a new car. By June, the prototype was already being tested. This new team car, the M6A, was the first McLaren sports car to feature a monocoque chassis and only three were built. The body was designed with a wedge-shaped front section to increase frontal downforce. A small block, fuel-injected, 360-cid Chevrolet engine that produced approximately 525-brake horsepower powered the M6A. A Hewland five-speed transmission and three rubber fuel cells with a total capacity of 65 gallons also equipped the car.

The whole package was presented in what was to become the most famous, and most remembered, paint scheme of the Can-Am era—McLaren Orange. All of the off-season hard work paid off as the M6A racked up five victories in the six races on the Can-Am schedule. Bruce McLaren had cinched his first Can-Am championship while teammate Denis Hulme finished second in the championship points.

The customer cars for 1967 were improved M1Bs that were marketed by Trojan as the M1C or the Mk. 3. A feature of most of the U.S. cars was a movable spoiler. There were 25 of these production models built, and most of them were used in the USRRC and the Can-Am series.

The 1967 USRRC series was completely dominated by Mark Donohue in his Sunoco Lola T70. Donohue won six of the eight races; McLaren customers (Motschenbacher at Laguna Seca and Chuck Parsons and Skip Scott at the Road America 500) won the other two.

In spite of Donohue's USRRC domination, by the time the 1967 race season was over, the McLaren team had served notice. They were poised and ready to take command of the race scene.

Lothar Motschenbacher (left) doesn't realize just how serious the lady fan in the center is.

John Cannon's (62) Genie, Lothar Motschenbacher's (27) McLaren Mk. 2, and Bud Morley's (6) McLaren Mk. 2 lead Jerry Hansen's (44) Lotus 19, Ronnie Bucknum's (51) Lola T70, Stan Burnett's (61) Chev. Mk. II, Ken Miles' (34) Porsche 906, Scooter Patrick's (33) Porsche 906, Charlie Hayes' (97) McLaren Mk. 2, and Jerry Entin's McLaren Mk. 1 to the first turn during the May 1966 Laguna Seca USRRC.

*My first year racing as a full-time professional was in 1966, and that was also when I bought my first McLaren. My first race with the new McLaren Mk. 2 was at the Riverside USRRC in April, and we had problems in practice and qualifying. I had to start well back in the field, but I moved up quickly to lead the race. Unfortunately, I blew the engine in the final laps and didn't finish. I was especially happy that I was able to lead the race my first time out because driving a car like that was a totally different driving experience for me.—*LOTHAR MOTSCHENBACHER

Charlie Hayes (97) won the first USRRC race for McLaren at Laguna Seca. Hayes was never lower then third place during the race and went on to an uncontested win.

Chris Amon (29) and Bruce McLaren (28), both driving McLaren M1Bs, finished second and third, in this order, at the International Trophy Race at Silverstone in May 1966. The 1966 British Group 7 season was completely dominated by Denis Hulme and John Surtees driving the rival Lola T70s.

Bruce McLaren's (4) McLaren M1B takes an early lead in the June 1966 Players 200 over Charlie Hayes' (97) McLaren Mk. 2, Chris Amon's (2) McLaren M1B, Jerry Grant's (8) Lola T70, John Cannon's (62) Genie, and Chuck Parsons' (80) Genie. McLaren won the race.

Lothar Motschenbacher (11) is on his way to a well-deserved second place at the Players 200. Tom Payne's (13) Cobra 427 trails Motschenbacher. "We ran a 305-cid Traco Oldsmobile engine in our Mk. 2, and it was basically the same engine that Bruce (McLaren) and Chris (Amon) were running in their cars. At Mosport, I blew up the only engine that I had after qualifying fifth, and I was ready to load up and go home. I knew that Bruce had a spare engine, and I also knew that he was staying in the same hotel that I was. I walked down to the lake where he was getting ready to go water skiing and, when he saw me, he said, 'I want it back tomorrow night.' I never had to ask him for the use of that engine, he just knew what I needed and he knew that I didn't have the money to pay for it. We installed the engine the next morning, and I finished second to Bruce in the race. We beat Chris Amon, who finished third, and we were the only car to finish on the same lap as Bruce. Immediately after the race, we pulled the engine out of the car and returned it to Bruce. It was still warm when we loaded it into his truck and the only thing that I did pay for was the engine rebuild that was done at Traco."—Lothar Motschenbacher

*Bruce would always come over and look at my car, as he did with most of the other independent drivers. I was rather in the dark when it came to chassis settings and tuning and, since Bruce obviously knew more about the cars than I did, I never hesitated to ask him questions. He would make recommendations and share things with me, and I learned a great deal from him.*—LOTHAR MOTSCHENBACHER

Bruce McLaren, Teddy Mayer, and Tyler Alexander take a victory lap after Bruce won the Players 200 at Mosport. This win capped a very successful week in Canada for the McLaren team because McLaren also won the Labatt 50 at St. Jovite the week before.

Bruce McLaren (left) and Chris Amon (right) celebrate their victory at Le Mans with Henry Ford II. It had been a long haul for the Ford Le Mans program, but finally it all came together in 1966.

Lothar Motschenbacher (in the striped shirt at the front of the car) helps prepare his Oldsmobile-powered McLaren Mk. 2 for the June 1966 Watkins Glen United States Road Racing Club (USRRC). Lothar DNF'ed when he blew the engine during the race.

By the time that the USRRC series moved to Mid-Ohio in August 1966, Lothar Motschenbacher had decided to cast his lot with the Nickey Chevrolet team and, with Chevrolet power, he finished, and won, his first race of the season.

*This was a season of trials and tribulations for us. I really liked the car, and we did reasonably well considering the budget that I had to work with.*—LOTHAR MOTSCHENBACHER

Also by the end of the 1966 USRRC season, Chuck Parsons switched to a McLaren Mk. 2, won the Road America 500, and wrapped up the series championship.

When the drivers and racing teams gathered at *Le Circuit Mont Tremblant–St. Jovite* in French-speaking Canada, 90 miles north of Montreal for the inaugural race of Can-Am series, the McLaren team appeared, for the first time on the North American continent, with Chevrolet engines powering their M1B team cars. Here, Tyler Alexander (left) and Bruce McLaren enjoy a relaxing moment prior to the start of the first practice session.

As an intrepid photographer captures Chris Amon and Masten Gregory (upper left) on film, the McLaren crew performs last-minute changes to Amon's M1B prior to the start of the September 1966 St. Jovite Can-Am. Chris Amon's brilliant charge through the field after a first lap pit stop to fix a sticking throttle and tear off a damaged front spoiler was the highlight of the meeting. Amon finished third overall.

Two of the most consistent performers in the USRRC display their skills in the Can-Am. Skip Scott (91) and Bud Morley (6), both in McLaren Mk. 2s, race for position early in the race. Morley finished ninth and Scott only completed four laps due to broken transmission linkage.

Sam Posey chose a McLaren Mk. 2 and a Ford engine for his first venture into the Can-Am series, and, according to Posey, it was the wrong choice. Posey finished 21st at St. Jovite after a blown engine put him out of the running late in the race.

Tyler Alexander signals Bruce McLaren that he is just two seconds behind John Surtees. Note Alexander's offbeat spelling of McLaren's name.

> *When I was choosing a car for the Can-Am series, I had my choice between a Lola and a McLaren, and I chose the McLaren. I was also given the choice between a Ford and a Chevrolet engine, and I chose the Ford. It soon became obvious to me that I made the wrong choice in both departments. The early McLarens were terrible cars, and you could never get the parts that you needed to upgrade them so that you could compete with the Lola T70s. The Ford engine was a complete disaster and could not compete with the Chevrolet.—*SAM POSEY

John Surtees nips Bruce McLaren for the St. Jovite win after a close race that had the crowd on its feet for the entire 203-mile event. The Can-Am series was off to a good start!

The beautifully prepared team McLaren M1Bs sit in the paddock prior to the start of the 1966 Bridgehampton Can-Am.

Bruce McLaren sits in his M1B prior to the beginning of practice at Bridgehampton. Chris Amon (left) and Tyler Alexander (center) talk to McLaren as Teddy Mayer keeps his eye on the competition.

Chris Amon talks to Teddy Mayer as Bruce McLaren (left) leans in to listen.

Can't you hear all of that wonderful noise as Dan Gurney's (30) Lola T70, John Surtees' (7) Lola T70, Bruce McLaren's (4) McLaren M1B, Chris Amon's (5) McLaren M1B, and Phil Hill's (66) Chaparral 2E lead the field away from the starting line at Bridgehampton?

If it were baseball, we would just call it the Squeeze Play, but it's motor racing at its very best, so we call it Great Racing. Battling for position during the opening laps of the Bridgehampton Cam Am are Chuck Parsons' (10) McLaren Mk. 2, Jerry Grant's (8) Lola T70, Parnelli Jones' (98) Lola T70, Masten Gregory's (88) McLaren Mk. 2, John Cannon's (62) McLaren Mk. 2, George Alderman's (23) Lola T70, Bud Morley's (61) McLaren Mk. 2, and Lothar Motschenbacher's (96) McLaren Mk. 2

Once again, Chris Amon's (5) McLaren M1B, lapping John Ryan's (36) Genie Mk. 10B and Earl Jones' (85) Elva Mk. 8-BMW put on a spectacular show for the large crowd. Amon made a big move to try and win the race during the closing laps, but it wasn't enough. He was narrowly beaten to the finish by Dan Gurney's Lola.

Bruce McLaren (right) gets a chuckle out of Tyler Alexander's joke as the team prepares for practice at Mosport. Chris Amon appears in the back with the white shirt.

Earl Jones wins the 25-lap BEMC Fall Classic on the day prior to the Mosport Can-Am. Jones was driving a McLaren Mk. 2.

At its peak, Can-Am meant great drivers, great cars, great atmosphere, and great circuits. This was sports car racing as it once was. Here Dan Gurney's (30) Lola T70, Chris Amon's (5) McLaren M1B, Bruce McLaren's (4) McLaren M1B, Sam Posey's (33) McLaren Mk. 2, and Denis Hulme (81) lead the charge to the first corner as the Mosport Can-Am begins.

An interesting variety of racing lines can be seen during the opening laps of the Mosport Can-Am. Chuck Parsons' (10) McLaren Mk. 2, Paul Hawkins' (11) Lola T70, Ludwig Heimrath's (39) McLaren Mk. 2, Masten Gregory's (88) McLaren Mk. 2, George Alderman's (23) Lola T70, Mak Kronn's (77) McKee, Ed Hamill's (60) Hamill SR3, Richard Brown's (38) McLaren Mk. 2, and Earl Jones' (99) McLaren Mk. 2 are all jockeying for position as John Cordts' (57) McLaren Mk. 1 chooses not to get too close.

As a large crowd of spectators gathers in the background, Lothar Motschenbacher surveys the damage from a first lap collision.

Chris Amon's (5) McLaren M1B, Dan Gurney's (30) Lola T70, and Bruce McLaren's (4) McLaren M1B spent most of the Mosport race swapping the first three positions. None of the three finished, however. Amon and McLaren both retired with suspension problems, and Gurney lost power 10 laps from victory. Mark Donohue won the race.

This photograph demonstrates what I have been saying for years: There was never a better place from which to shoot the start of a race than at Laguna Seca. From this position (sadly long gone), one could get the entire field in the picture in a way that could not be done anywhere else. Jim Hall's (66) Chaparral 2E, Phil Hill's (65) Chaparral 2E, Bruce McLaren's (4) McLaren M1B, John Surtees' (7) Lola T70, Masten Gregory's (88) McLaren Mk. 2, Mark Donohue's (61) Lola T70, Denis Hulme's (8) Lola T70, John Cannon's (62) McLaren Mk. 2, Chris Amon's (5) McLaren M1B, Earl Jones' (99) McLaren Mk. 2, Bill Eve's (52) Genie Mk. 10, and Pedro Rodriguez's (21) Ferrari Dino lead the rest of the field away from the start.

Bruce McLaren deep in concentration at Laguna Seca. At his race, Jim Hall's winged Chaparral 2E and John Surtees' Lola T70 posed the greatest threats to Bruce's M1B.

John Cannon's (62) McLaren Mk. 2 and Mike Goth (86) are lapped by Bruce McLaren (4) at Laguna Seca. Cannon finished fifth overall, Goth blew an engine, and McLaren finished third overall.

Bruce McLaren's (4) McLaren M1B and Jim Hall's (66) Chaparral 2E battle for second position as John Cannon's (62) McLaren Mk. 2 lurks in the background. At Laguna Seca, McLaren was able to stay extremely competitive with the Chaparral due to an experimental fuel-injected engine.

By the time that the Can-Am series moved to Riverside, the McLaren team had made some major upgrades to Bruce McLaren's car. Although not seen here, a movable spoiler was installed on the rear body section and a 5.9-liter, fuel-injected Chevrolet engine was installed in the engine bay. A number of spectators gathered in the garage area as team members prepare the car for practice. Bruce McLaren and Chris Amon can be seen in the upper right of the picture.

Bruce McLaren is all business as he qualifies for the pole position during the October 1966 Riverside Can-Am.

*I really respected Bruce's engineering ability. He was one of those people who were, what I call, a practical engineer. He was not a classroom engineer but, like many of the people in racing at that time, he had a great deal of common sense and he was very straightforward.*—LOTHAR MOTSCHENBACHER

Chris Amon qualifies in seventh position for the Riverside Can-Am.

When the green flag fell to start the Riverside Can-Am, Bruce McLaren (4) took an immediate lead over Jim Hall's (66) Chaparral 2E and John Surtees' (7) Lola T70.

McLaren (4) led the first 10 laps of the race before his engine gave out, and he was sidelined for the duration. Sam Posey's (33) McLaren Mk. 2 trails McLaren into Riverside's Turn 7.

Masten Gregory had been an outstanding international driver for many years when he came to drive in the 1966 Can-Am series. Gregory won the consolation race and started in the middle of the field, but he was black-flagged 20 laps into the race because he was unable to maintain competitive speed.

Chris Amon didn't have much luck at Riverside, and he retired with a dead battery after 50 laps.

John Cannon was always one of the fastest of the independent McLaren competitors in 1966. His luck wasn't good at Riverside, however, and he retired after six laps with a blown engine.

By the time that the Can-Am entered the final race of the 1966 season, the McLaren team had re-installed carburetors on both Amon's and McLaren's engines.

Bruce McLaren's (4) McLaren M1B and Dan Gurney (30) are in a close race for second place during the early laps of the Las Vegas Can-Am. Gurney retired with a fuel leak, and McLaren went on to finish second overall. As good as the M1Bs were, they were not good enough to beat the Lola T70s in 1966.

When the McLaren team decided to pass on the annual Nassau Speedweeks in December 1966, challenging the Lolas and Chaparrals was left up to the top North American independent McLaren teams. Brett Lunger, driving a McLaren Mk. 2 (18), finished second to Hap Sharp's Chaparral 2E in the Governor's Trophy.

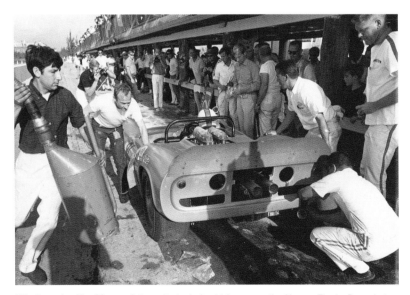

Skip Scott (making his mandatory pit stop) should have won the Nassau Trophy Race, but an off-course excursion on the last lap cost Scott the race. Mark Donohue was the winner and Scott finished second.

Bruce McLaren's 1967 season started off in fine style with a win in the new Ford Mk. IV at Sebring. Mario Andretti, being interviewed by Bob Holbert, was McLaren's co-driver.

The 1967 USRRC season started in April at Las Vegas. Mark Donohue (6) and George Follmer (16), both in Lola T70s, lead Skip Scott (91), Peter Revson (52), and Chuck Parsons (10), all in McLaren Mk. 2s, into the first corner. Donohue won the race and none of the McLaren drivers finished.

When the USRRC moved to Riverside during the last week of April, Mark Donohue (6) and George Follmer (16) once again had their Lola T70s in the front row while Peter Revson (52), Lothar Motschenbacher (11), Bob Bondurant (61), Bud Morley (71), and Skip Scott (91) put their McLaren Mk. 2s in the starting positions just behind the Lolas. Jerry Grant's (78) Lola T70 is also seen in the picture. Bondurant finished second to Donohue, while Motschenbacher finished third. Scott, Morley, and Revson failed to finish.

Skip Scott (91) laps a slower car during the April 1967 USRRC at Las Vegas.

Close racing between Peter Revson (52) and Skip Scott (91), both driving McLaren Mk. 2s, was one of the highlights of the Laguna Seca USRRC. Unfortunately, neither of these top-notch drivers finished.

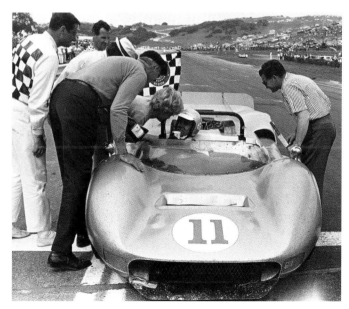

Lothar Motschenbacher (11) won the first USRRC race for the McLaren marque at Laguna Seca in May 1967. Motschenbacher's wife, Marilyn, can be seen congratulating him.

Some of the great cars and drivers that gathered for the June 1967 Watkins Glen USRRC are seen in this photo taken prior to the start. Chuck Parsons (26), John Cannon (62), Lothar Motschenbacher (11), Peter Revson (52), and Bob Bondurant (51) are all in McLaren Mk. 2s. Lining up behind the leaders are Skip Hudson's (9) McKee, Mike Goth's (14) Lola T70, Donald Morin's (36) McLaren Mk. 3, Ludwig Heimrath's (39) McLaren Mk. 2, Skip Barber's (44) Lola T70, Bud Morley's (13) McLaren Mk. 2, and Charlie Kolb's (21) Lola T70. Shortly after this photograph was taken, Bob Bondurant was involved in a spectacular near fatal accident.

> *I reached over and shut off the fuel pump, shut off the ignition, and said to myself, 'Shit, Bondurant, this is going to be a bad one.'* — BOB BONDURANT

Lothar Motschenbacher (11) and Skip Scott (91), both in McLaren Mk. 2s, battle for third place at the Kent, Washington, USRRC. Motschenbacher finished third, and Scott failed to finish.

# BOB BONDURANT'S WILD RIDE

"After three years of mostly racing in Europe, I decided to stay in the U.S. and race in the popular Group 7 USRRC and Can-Am series. I teamed with Peter Revson to drive for Peyton Cramer's Dana Chevrolet team in those two series. We were to receive two new Lolas, but they never materialized. We both wound up driving two older McLaren Mk. 2s that were really shit boxes. Those cars were not very reliable and we could never really get them to work properly. One of the biggest problems was that it [was] impossible to get the latest pieces from McLaren because, as a nonfactory driver, you always got last year's parts. We both tried very hard, but those cars could not keep up with the Lolas, no matter how hard you drove them.

"By the time we got to the Glen, my car wasn't working worth a damn and I had my worst qualifying position of the season there. Nothing seemed to be right that weekend and early in the race the steering broke. This happened on one of the fastest parts of the track were I was running in the 150-mile-per-hour range. I went into a huge slide and struck a 3- or 4-foot dirt embankment where the track was preparing to install a guardrail, and that launched me up into the trees. It's amazing what you think about at a time like that because it all seems to be happening in slow motion. I reached over and shut off the fuel pump, shut off the ignition, and said to myself, 'Shit, Bondurant, this is going to be a bad one.' People told me that the car flew as high as a telephone pole. I went end over end and barrel-rolled eight times, and I remember seeing the tree tops next to the track. The car was completely disintegrated by the time that it stopped rolling. When I was launched off the banking, the aluminum floorpan of the McLaren was torn away and that exposed my feet and legs to the ground every time I flipped or rolled. Looking back at it, I was lucky that my legs and feet didn't get torn off.

"I flipped down half of the front straight and landed upside down. The fact that it had rained the previous night, and that the ground was soft, probably saved my life. When the corner workers turned what was left of the car over, I noticed how close I came to landing in a spectator area.

"I passed out and woke up in the hospital. I was told by the doctors that I had broken both ankles, crushed both feet, had several broken ribs, a broken left leg, taken a chip out of a vertebra, and a chunk out of my forehead. I was also told that I was very fortunate not to be paralyzed, and that I would probably never walk again. That really scared me because I had always been a very active person. Lying in the hospital gives you a lot of time to think, and I realized that I had to go on and make a living and that racing was what I knew best. It was during that time in the hospital that I decided if I could get back on my feet again, I would start a driving school. Over the next week, I took a yellow pad and put together most of the basic school curriculum that I still use today. It was during the time that I was undergoing my rehabilitation that I physically got the school going and, in time, I was also able to return to racing.—Bob Bondurant

Bruce McLaren discusses the results of a Goodwood M6A with Teddy Mayer (left) test prior to the start of the 1967 Can-Am season.

Did the new car work? Figure it out for yourself as McLaren and his new teammate Denis Hulme were 10 seconds under the previous lap record during the opening round of the Can-Am season at Road America.

Another fellow New Zealander, Denis Hulme, replaced Chris Amon, who had signed with Ferrari, for the 1967 season. In addition to driving Group 7 cars for McLaren, Hulme was at the top of the heap in the points chase for the F1 World Championship driving a Brabham. Can't you see that happening now?

Denny Hulme and Don Beresford (on shoulders of fellow mechanic) celebrate the McLaren team's first Can-Am victory at Road America in September 1967. Stirling Moss conducts the postrace interview. From September 1967 through August 1974, the McLaren-built cars won an unbelievable total of 43 races in the Can-Am series.

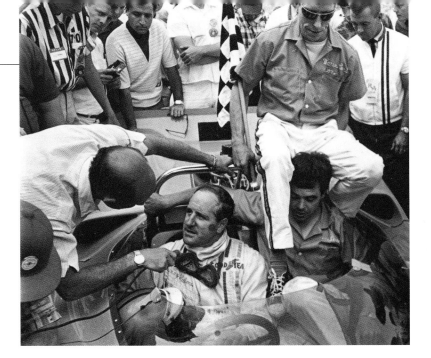

Mario Andretti (left) and Bruce McLaren must be reminiscing about their Ford Mk. IV win at Sebring.

The first lap at Bridgehampton has Dennis Hulme's (5) McLaren M6A pulling away from a strong field that included Bruce McLaren's (4) McLaren M6A and Mark Donohue's (6) Lola T70. The McLaren teammates also had the two fastest qualifying times, with Hulme winning the pole position.

Second-place finisher Bruce McLaren (left) pours some bubbly for winner Denis Hulme (right) at Bridgehampton. This was the second consecutive one-two finish for the McLaren team, and they certainly seem to be enjoying their newly found success.

Bruce wonders if everything is ready to go at Mosport.

Before the race at Mosport, McLaren (left), Stirling Moss (center), and Denny Hulme (right) enjoy a light piece of commentary in the local newspaper.

Although he only qualified in second position, McLaren (4), along with Hulme, broke Jim Clark's F1 qualifying record by almost two seconds.

After a late start because of a fuel leak, McLaren gave the Mosport crowd something to cheer about as he cut through the field toward Dan Gurney (36), who was running in second place. After several laps of running together, McLaren got by Gurney to capture second.

Chuck Parsons' (26) McLaren M1C leads Mark Donohue's (6) Lola T70 at Mosport. Parsons and Donohue both failed to finish because of blown engines.

Denny Hulme was the fastest of the fast at Mosport.

Late in the race, Skip Scott's (91) McLaren M1C is lapped by the hard-driving Bruce McLaren. Scott finished seventh and McLaren finished second.

After Mosport, Denny Hulme was three for three in the win column. Could it get any better?

Tyler Alexander and crew push McLaren's car to the starting grid after the Can-Am series moved west to Laguna Seca.

At Laguna Seca, Bruce McLaren's (4) McLaren M6A starts on the pole with Dan Gurney's (36) Lola T70 next to him. Parnelli Jones' (21) Lola T70, Denny Hulme's (5) McLaren M6A, Mike Spence's (22) McLaren Mk. 2, Jim Hall's (66) Chaparral 2G, Charlie Hayes' (25) McKee Mk. 7, and Lothar Motschenbacher's (11) Lola T70 are behind the front row.

Denny Hulme (5) laps Brett Lunger's (2) McLaren Mk. 2 at Laguna Seca. Hulme suffered the team's first DNF of the year when his engine blew on lap 80.

Denny won the first three; now it's Bruce's turn. McLaren wins his first Can-Am at Laguna Seca.

An engine change was in order prior to the start of the *Times* Grand Prix at Riverside.

The powerful McLaren team, McLaren (4) and Hulme (5), drew a crowd wherever it went in 1967. Here the team prepares to qualify at Riverside.

Hulme's race was over almost before it started as he pitted to have repairs made after Parnelli Jones' Lola kicked up a loose tire marker at Turn 8. After repairs were completed, Hulme tried to re-enter the race but was prevented from doing so by officials who thought the body damage was too great.

One of the great Can-Am races of the entire series occurred at Riverside when Bruce McLaren's (4) McLaren M6A and Jim Hall's (66) Chaparral 2G exchanged the lead numerous times before McLaren pulled out to a three-second lead to win the race.

Denny Hulme (center) and Bruce McLaren (behind Hulme) take a few moments to relax, talk to fans, and answer a few reporter questions before the Stardust Grand Prix at Las Vegas in November 1967.

Denny Hulme (5) and Bruce McLaren (4) are near the front as the field led by Parnelli Jones' (21) Lola T70 heads for Turn 1. Also visible are Peter Revson's (52) Lola T70, Jim Hall's (66) Chaparral 2G, and Dan Gurney's (36) Lola T70.

Even though McLaren's race was over (blown engine) after 21 laps, he still won his first Can-Am championship at Las Vegas. Note the oil on McLaren's helmet.

Denny Hulme (5) had his chance to win the Can-Am championship at Las Vegas, but his engine also blew. Hulme finished second in the Can-Am championship in addition to winning the 1967 F1 World Championship. Mark Donohue's (6) Lola T70 almost won the race but ran out of gas on the last lap, giving the win to John Surtees.

# CHAPTER 4

# THE BRUCE AND DENNY SHOW

## 1968

The 1968 season was a good one for the McLaren marque. Mark Donohue won the championship in what was to be the final year of the USRRC. Donohue blitzed his way to the championship by driving the M6A that Roger Penske had purchased from Bruce McLaren following McLaren's 1967 Cam Am championship. By 1968, interest had waned in the USRRC, and the entry list of drivers and teams had shrunk considerably. With many of the name drivers competing in other series, the promoters were not willing to take the risk of putting on a race without knowing that the top teams and drivers would definitely appear for their event. This sealed the fate of the six-year-old series.

Even though there were only six races on the Cam Am schedule for 1968, the series, now entering its third season, had found a niche with the fans. The sight, sound, and smell of 30 thundering, big-engine cars roaring into the first turn of a true road circuit was very addicting indeed. The 1968 season was a huge success for the McLaren marque as a car of that name would win all six of the races. Four wins went to the McLaren team (Bruce McLaren at Riverside and Hulme at Road America, Edmonton, and Las Vegas) and two went to private McLaren customers (Mark Donohue won at Bridgehampton and John Cannon at Laguna Seca).

The cars that McLaren and Hulme drove were brand new M8As, of which only three were built. These cars featured a lighter and wider monocoque chassis (to accommodate wider tires and larger fuel tanks), 74-gallon fuel tanks, four-speed Hewland LG500 gearboxes, and 427-ci, aluminum Chevrolet engines. The 1968 customer McLaren car was called the M6B; the production version of the championship was the M6A. This car was in tremendous demand by the USRRC and Can-Am competitors, and 28 of them were built and sold almost as fast as they could be produced.

The beautifully prepared Penske Racing Sunoco McLaren M6A, with Mark Donohue driving, completely dominated the 1968 USRRC Championship.

The first USRRC race of the 1968 season was held in Mexico City, and it was won by well-known Mexican driver Moises Solana. Solana (9) drove a McLaren M6B to that win. This picture, taken at Riverside, shows Solana, who finished fifth, leading John Cannon's (62) McLaren Mk. 2 and Chuck Parsons' (10) Lola T70 into Turn 7.

The top of Turn 6 at Riverside was one of my favorite photographic spots for many reasons. This picture, with Mark Donohue's (6) McLaren M6A leading the entire USRRC field through the esses, illustrates one of the many reasons why that spot was so loved by the many photographers who were track regulars. Donohue, who won the race, leads Lothar Motschenbacher's (11) McLaren M6B, Peter Revson's (52) Lola T70, Skip Scott's (26) Lola T70, Sam Posey's (1) Caldwell D7B, and Moises Solana's (9) McLaren M6B on the first lap. Motschenbacher finished second and Posey finished third.

Mark Donohue's (6) McLaren M6A, Sam Posey's (1) Caldwell D7B, Lothar Motschenbacher's (11) McLaren M6B, and John Cannon's (62) McLaren Mk. 2 prepare to start the Watkins Glen USRRC in July 1968.

Roger Penske (left) and Mark Donohue (right) discuss the potential of their new, highly modified McLaren M6B after a successful test at Bridgehampton in August 1968. This car had reworked suspension, the body had been lightened and reconfigured, and the Chevrolet 427-ci aluminum Chevrolet was built by Traco.

The M8A goes together at the McLaren factory. The entire rear third of the car is filled by the engine and transmission.

The 1968 team cars prepare to leave Colinbrook for the upcoming 1968 Can-Am season. Note the 1965 Ford Fairlane wagon pulling McLaren's (4) car.

The first race of the year was at Road America in September. Denny Hulme (left) watches as the crew makes final changes to the car before practice begins. Note the air intake for the radiator and brake cooling.

Early in the race, Jim Hall (66), Chaparral 2G, and Denny Hulme battle for the lead at Road America. Denny qualified second and won the race. Hall finished fifth.

Tyler Alexander prepares to signal McLaren that he is 26 seconds ahead of Mario Andretti and 39 seconds ahead of Mark Donohue.

Bruce McLaren was a fast qualifier and second overall. It was a different year, but the final results were still the same.

The wedge-style bodywork on the M8A is evident at Bridgehampton.

*The M6B was a good car, but we completely reworked the one that we got and called it the McLeagle. We managed to screw up the suspension so badly that the car never did work properly, and our results with it were much less than we hoped for.—DAN GURNEY*

Bruce McLaren (4) and Denny Hulme (5), both in M8As, lead Peter Revson's (52) McLaren M6B, Mark Donohue's (6) McLaren M6B, Jim Hall's (66) Chaparral 2G, Dan Gurney's (48) McLeagle-Ford, and John Surtees' (7) Lola T160 during the first lap at Bridgehampton. Both team McLarens blew their engines, leaving the door open to the independents.

Jim Hall's (66) Chaparral 2G chases down Dan Gurney's (48) McLeagle-Ford at Bridgehampton. Gurney finished seventh, and Hall, the star of the day, finished second.

Jo Bonnier participated in the full Can-Am series for the first, and only, time in 1968. Bonnier's M6B was hampered by engine problems and seldom finished. The Bonnier McLaren had a best finish of eighth overall at Las Vegas.

George Eaton was another longtime independent McLaren competitor. In 1968, Eaton campaigned a McLaren Mk. 3 and had a best finish of third overall at Laguna Seca.

When you have the best team and the best cars it's very easy to relax during a break in the action. Bruce McLaren catches up on the latest automotive news at Edmonton.

Denny Hulme prepares to start the race as the two team McLarens sit in the front row at Edmonton.

Mark Donohue (6), Peter Revson (52), and Dan Gurney (48), all in M6Bs, race trough the esses at Edmonton. Donohue finished third behind the team cars, while Revson and Gurney didn't finish.

The extensive rear-body modifications to the Sunoco McLaren M6B are visible here.

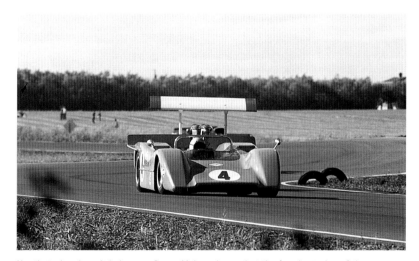

No, that wing doesn't belong on Bruce McLaren's car, but the foreshortening of the camera lens makes it look like it does. McLaren, who finished second, leads Jim Hall's winged-Chaparral at Edmonton.

Lothar Motschenbacher's (11) McLaren M12 leads Ron Bucknum's (31) Lola T70 at Edmonton. Neither finished the race.

Teddy Mayer holds the stopwatches as Tyler Alexander prepares to tell McLaren that Peter Revson is out of the race.

Denny Hulme wins at Edmonton.

It was far from ideal driving conditions when the Can-Am series came to Laguna Seca in October 1968, but that didn't keep the race from running!

Peter Revson's (52) McLaren M6B, Jerry Entin's (12) Lola T70, Denny Hulme's (5) McLaren M8A, Mark Donohue's (6) McLaren M8A, and George Follmer's (34) Lola T70 pick their way cautiously down the Corkscrew during the Laguna Seca downpour. Revson, Hulme, and Donohue all led the race at some point in time, but they all ran into various problems due to the rain.

Pole-sitter Bruce McLaren (4), McLaren M8A, and Mark Donohue (6), McLaren M6B, round Turn 9 in the pouring rain. McLaren finished fifth and Donohue finished eighth. Note that McLaren's goggles are missing. Both McLaren and later Donohue were plagued throughout the race with goggles that continuously fogged up.

*It was definitely one of those days when things didn't go according to plan and a smaller engine had a definite advantage over the bigger, more powerful ones.*—JOHN CANNON

John Cannon (62) and his three-year-old McLaren Mk. 2 were the stars of the day. Cannon's choice of Firestone rain tires gave him the advantage that he needed to score one of the biggest upsets in the Can-Am series. Cannon laps Brian O'Neil's (15) Lola T70 on his way to the win.

Denny Hulme probably wishes he had pontoons on his M8A rather than tires as he tries, in vain, to catch the flying John Cannon.

John Cannon scored one of the most popular wins in sports car racing history at Laguna Seca.

## THE DAY CANNON SLAYED THE GIANT

"To this day, I remember every moment of that race. On Sunday morning, I knew that unless I did something really stupid that I could win the race. I knew this because I had done a lot of tire testing for Firestone, and they gave me a lot of support in the way of tires at the races. I had tested rain tires for Firestone the previous year, and I knew how good those tires were, and I also knew that, because of the weather, this was going to be my big opportunity.

"I'd always said to the other guys, somewhat arrogantly I guess, that if I ever had an equal car, I would beat them all. During the Sunday morning warm-ups in the rain, I was two seconds faster than the rest of the field, and when I pulled in, Chris Economaki came over to me and said, 'Bruce [McLaren] tells me that you are the dark horse in this race.' I told Chris, 'If this rain keeps up, I will win.' Chris just looked at me in a strange manner. Once the race started, I went absolutely on the limit, flat out, because I felt that the rain was going to let up and that the track was going to dry out. I drove like a bloody demon, because I figured that if I had a big enough lead, and the rain stopped, that I could afford to give up a couple of seconds a lap to the bigger boys and still win the race.

"During that race I had tremendous confidence in my equipment and I was able to pass people at will. I lapped the entire field and beat Denny Hulme's factory McLaren by a lap. It was definitely one of those days when things didn't go according to plan and a smaller engine had a definite advantage over the bigger, more powerful ones."—John Cannon

As McLaren (4) prepares to qualify at Riverside, Hulme (in helmet at right) watches last-minute preparations. Bruce was the fastest qualifier, with Denny sitting next to him in second position.

In the early laps of the Riverside Can-Am, "the Bruce and Denny Show" —finally free from past engine problems—pull out to a big lead over the rest of the field.

Jerry Hansen (44), in the M6A that won the 1967 Cam Am title with Bruce McLaren and the 1968 USRRC championship with Mark Donohue, leads John Cannon's (62) McLaren M1B and Swede Savage's (36) McLeagle at Turn 7. Hansen finished seventh, Cannon finished sixth, and Savage finished eighth.

In the late laps of the race, Denny Hulme ran off the road to avoid a back marker and, for the second year in a row, damaged a front fender in the process. In spite of two pit stops for repairs, Hulme still managed a fifth-place finish.

Bruce McLaren liked Riverside and, since 1961, most always had good results there. In October 1968, he achieved his second win in a row at the *L.A. Times* Grand Prix. McLaren holds the Johnson Wax Can-Am Championship Trophy (which actually belonged to Hulme) while Tyler holds the *L.A. Times* trophy. It was the second year that the McLaren team would win the championship. There would be three more to follow.

Denny Hulme (5) leads the field into the first turn at the November 1968 Stardust Grand Prix. Bruce McLaren (4), Jim Hall (66) and his Chaparral 2G, Dan Gurney (48) and his Lola T160, Sam Posey (1) and his Lola T160, and Peter Revson (52) and his McLaren M6B are also up front. Hulme won this and two other races during the 1968 season, clinching his first of two Can-Am Championships.

The M8A of Denny Hulme sits on a London street before a horde of onlookers in late 1968. Note the signage on the nose stating "McLaren Cars, Can Am Champion 1967 & 1968."

# CHAPTER 5

# THE
# PERFECT SEASON

By 1969, the Can-Am series had reached its zenith with 11 races scheduled and a $1 million unlimited sports car racing championship. Professional sports car racing had certainly come a long way since its humble beginnings in 1958. What has been completely overlooked by many of the so-called experts who produce numerous published lists of the "Greatest Motor Sports Accomplishments" is the fact that the McLaren team had a perfect season, winning 11 out of 11 Can-Am races in 1969. Not only did the team win all 11 races, they had 8 one-two finishes and, in one instance, a one-two-three finish at Michigan.

There was no question by 1969 that McLaren was the best-prepared team in the Can-Am series. Many other factories had promised teams and support for the series, but when it materialized, if at all, it was a half-hearted, lackluster effort. Only Lola in 1966, Chaparral from 1966 to 1970, and Porsche in 1972 and 1973 rivaled the McLaren effort.

The question must be asked: Did McLaren's domination of the series discourage other factories from coming aboard? Many of the participants from the era say absolutely, it did. Most other racing operations and factories just didn't want to spend the money or the time to develop a car to rival the "Bruce and Denny Show." The McLaren factory realized early on that the money made in the Can-Am would help keep their doors open and even help fund their other projects in FI and USAC. Denny Hulme recalled, "We counted on the money that could be made in the Can-Am. If we didn't do well there, we were really in the shit for the rest of the year." McLaren's effort in the Can-Am was the type of professional commitment that was needed to be successful in that series, and their five-year domination there should never be questioned.

The M8B of the 1969 season was the first, and only, McLaren to finally incorporate the Chaparral-type rear airfoil that put the downforce onto the rear wheel hubs. The chassis was a modified version of

The ultimate McLaren weapon—the M8B—sits in the Colinbrook factory before shipment to North America.

the M8A, and the 430-ci aluminum Chevrolet put out a reported 680 horsepower. Three M8Bs were built, and on two occasions (Michigan and Laguna Seca) all three were raced. The production model for 1969 was called the M12, and it was based on the previous year's championship-winning M8A. In all, there were 12 M12s built.

Denny Hulme and Teddy Mayer both remarked in later years that the McLaren M8B was the best McLaren ever built, and raced, by the team. Both Hulme and Mayer said, "How could anyone possibly argue with the record?"

It looks years ahead of its time, which wasn't exactly true, but its performance record certainly put it in that category. The clean, functional lines, radiator and oil cooling ducts, and the Chaparral-style spoiler are readily visible here.

Colin Beanland, Tyler Alexander, and the rest of the McLaren crew enjoy a laugh before practice begins at Mosport, the first of 11 Can-Am races in 1969.

When your team is on top, everyone wants to ask the same silly questions.

Are Bruce and Denny discussing in what order they will finish?

John Surtees was supposed to drive a Chaparral in 1969, but when the season started and the car wasn't ready, the team bought a McLaren M12. As the season unfolded, Surtees preferred the M12 to the radical, unproven, and unsuccessful Chaparral 2H; but his idea of parking the Chaparral and concentrating on the M12 didn't sit well with Jim Hall. The McLaren was only run intermittently. At Mosport, Surtees qualified in the McLaren and finished third overall.

Bruce and Denny pick up from where they left off in 1968. It didn't matter who was in front; the McLaren domination of the 11-race season was absolute.

Every race demanded fine-tuning of the automobiles. Here, Denny discusses adjustments to the McLaren M8B's wing.

Dan Gurney broke the only Ford engine that he had available during practice at St. Jovite. Denny Hulme (right) attempts to humor the AAR mechanics while they try to salvage the day. The engine was found to have a broken piston, forcing the team to pack the car and return to California.

There's nothing like a little relaxation prior to the start of the St. Jovite race.

Bruce McLaren seems to be enjoying the new McLaren secret weapon that he found near the track. You will note that Bruce's friend comes complete with custom wing and decals.

The drivers usually get all of the recognition, but most of them will readily admit that, without a great crew, the car wouldn't get out of the garage. The professionalism of the McLaren crew is seen here. Every man knew his job and did it well.

It was a lot different in 1969 as far as the spectators were concerned. Unlike today, they were allowed to roam almost at will near the track and in the paddock.

As the race started, Bruce McLaren's (4) McLaren M8B took the lead from Chuck Parsons' (10) Lola T163, Denny Hulme's (5) McLaren M8B, Lothar Motschenbacher's (11) McLaren M12, Jerry Titus' (17) McLaren M1C, and Joe Leonard's (25) McKee Mk. 7. Note the large crowd in the stands above the pit boxes.

Lothar Motschenbacher's (11) McLaren M12, Chuck Parsons' (10) Lola T163, and George Eaton's (98) McLaren M12 battle for third place. Motschenbacher led the race in the early laps but gave way to the aster M8Bs and finished fourth. Parsons finished third while Eaton finished seventh.

John Surtees' (7) McLaren M12 and Bruce McLaren's (4) McLaren M8B swapped the lead numerous times during the first half of the race, but they collided when a back marker spun just before the pits. Both cars entered the pits for repairs and returned to the race. Surtees was eventually forced to retire when his heavily taped rear body panel broke apart and tore away.

Bruce McLaren, showing the effects of his collision with Surtees, came back to finish second.

Denny Hulme ran a clean race at St. Jovite to win his first race of the 1969 season.

Fred Baker (29), driving what looks like the ex-Sunoco McLaren M6B, leads Tom Dutton's (79) Lola T70 at St. Jovite. Baker finished sixth while Dutton finished Dutton finished 11th.

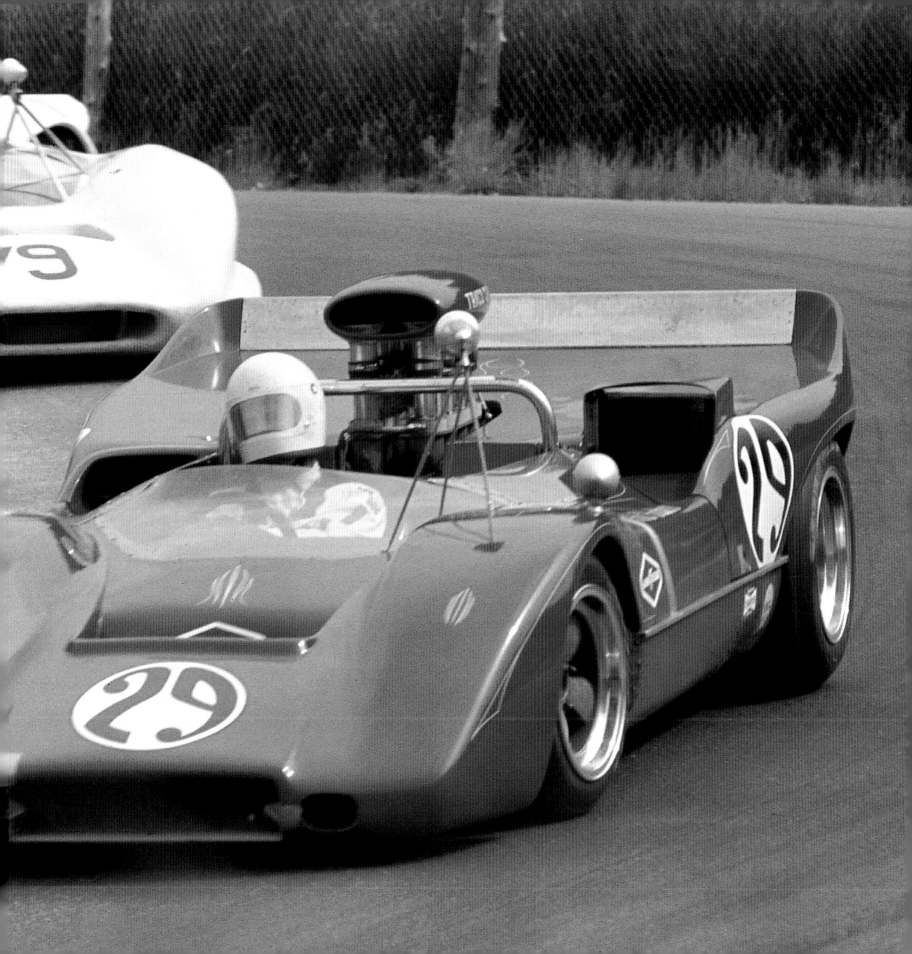

A top view, taken from the top of the pit boxes, of the M8B driven by Denny Hulme at Watkins Glen. The gas tanks mounted on each side of the driver are seen here, along with the brake and radiator cooling ducts.

The starting field at Watkins Glen was always an interesting one because many of the cars that had competed the FIA 6-Hour Race the day before, usually decided to try their luck in the Can-Am race also. Bruce McLaren (4) and Denny Hulme (5), both in McLaren M8Bs, are on the front row of the Watkins Glen Can-Am. Behind them are John Surtees' (7) McLaren M12, Chris Amon's (16) Ferrari 612, George Eaton's (98) McLaren M12, Lothar Motschenbacher's (11) McLaren M12, Chuck Parsons' (10) Lola T163, Fred Baker's (29) McLaren M6B, Jo Bonnier's (19) Lola T70 Mk. 3B, Jo Siffert's (1) Porsche 908, Brian Redman's (2) Porsche 908, John Cordts' (55) McLaren M6B, Ron Bucknum's (31) Lola T163, and Vic Elford's (14) Porsche 908.

The McLaren team, at full speed, crest the hill at Watkins Glen.

For the third race in a row, the McLaren team M8Bs finished one-two. It was great for the McLaren team treasury, and for the record book, but was the lack of quality competition really great for the sport?

Before suffering from engine problems, John Surtees' winged Chaparral McLaren M12 gave the team cars some much needed competition.

A jubilant Bruce McLaren enjoys his second win in three races at Watkins Glen.

The M8Bs of McLaren (4) and Hulme (5) line up on the front row at Edmonton. The Ferrari 612 (16) of Chris Amon and the McLaren M12 (98) of George Eaton are in the second row.

For the first time in a long time, another car, Chris Amon (16) in the Ferrari 612, actually led a Can-Am race. Amon's Ferrari, with its 6.2-liter engine, was extremely fast, but a serious lack of factory support doomed the project almost before the start. Amon finished second to Denny Hulme at Edmonton. "That Ferrari was very quick but sadly, the factory didn't really get behind the project. We could run close to the McLarens for a while, but the engines weren't reliable, and as the season wore on we couldn't finish the races. I always felt that Bruce and Denny toyed with me at Edmonton and let me lead the race to make it look like they finally had some competition."–Chris Amon

For the first time during the 1969 season, Bruce McLaren failed to finish a race when his engine blew on the 36th lap of the race at Edmonton.

Denny Hulme won the Edmonton race by 5.1 seconds over Chris Amon's Ferrari.

> *I always felt that Bruce and Denny toyed with me at Edmonton and let me lead the race to make it look like they finally had some competition.* –CHRIS AMON

George Eaton's (98) M12 finished in third place. Here, Eaton leads Chuck Parsons' (10) smoking Lola T163. Parsons retired with a water leak and fire on the 34th lap.

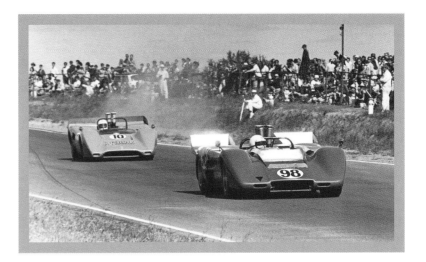

It seems as if the entire crowd at Edmonton gathered around the elevated victory stand to watch Denny Hulme celebrate his win.

When everything is going well, the tool and spare parts boxes can be used for a little rest period.

Once again, at Mid-Ohio, the M8Bs of McLaren (4) and Hulme (5) were on the front row. Falling in behind are Mark Donohue's (6) Lola T163, Chuck Parsons' (10) Lola T163, John Surtees' (7) Chaparral 2H, George Eaton's (98) McLaren M12, Jo Siffert's (0) Porsche 917PA, Peter Revson's (31) Lola T163, Lothar Motschenbacher's (11) McLaren M12, John Cannon's (99) McLaren M6B, Tony Dean's (9) Porsche 908, and Chris Amon's (16) Ferrari 612.

Is that concern showing on the faces of the McLaren crew? They need not worry. The two team cars finished one-two, with Hulme taking the win.

It seems like everyone was sprouting wings by the time the Can-Am series reached Bridgehampton. As usual, Bruce McLaren (4) and Denny Hulme (5), in their M8Bs, led from the start. Behind them are John Surtees' (7) Chaparral McLaren M12, Chris Amon's (16) Ferrari 612, George Eaton's (98) McLaren M12, Chuck Parsons' (10) Lola T163, Peter Revson's (31) Lola T163, Bob Dini's (75) Lola T162, Jo Siffert's (0) Porsche 917PA, and Lothar Motschenbacher's (11) McLaren M12.

Bruce McLaren laps Bill Wonder's (8) McLaren M8C on the fast Bridgehampton circuit. McLaren finished second behind Denny Hulme.

These signs appeared at Road America on the morning of the race. The McLaren crew prepared an answering sign that said, "Get Stuffed."

Denny Hulme
(left) watches
Bruce McLaren
prepare to qualify
at Michigan
International
Speedway.

*Bruce offered me his spare car and I jumped at the chance to drive the M8B. . . . What a great car to drive. That car was light-years ahead of the rest of the cars running in the Can-Am.*
—DAN GURNEY

The rolling start of the first, and last, Can-Am race ever to run at Michigan International Speedway finds Bruce McLaren's (4) McLaren M8B leading Denny Hulme's (5) McLaren M8B, Peter Revson's (31) Lola T163, Jo Siffert's (0) Porsche 917PA, George Eaton's (98) McLaren M12, Andrea de Adamich's (7) McLaren M12, and Chuck Parsons through the infield portion of what was primarily an oval track.

Dan Gurney (1) wound up driving the third McLaren M8B after the Chevrolet engine of his McLeagle gave up. Since he wasn't able to qualify the McLaren, Gurney had to start at the back of the pack. When the green flag fell, Dan moved quickly through the field until he was in third place behind the other two M8Bs. Here, Gurney passes eighth-place finisher George Eaton.

"I finally gave up on the Ford engines that never came, and I switched to the readily available Chevrolet. We had some problems with that engine at Michigan and parked the car after qualifying ninth. Bruce offered me his spare car and I jumped at the chance to drive the M8B. I started at the rear of the pack and was quickly able to move up to the front behind Bruce and Denny. What a great car to drive. That car was light years ahead of the rest of the cars running in the Can-Am at that time."—Dan Gurney

John Surtees was ill, keeping him out of the Michigan race, so he sent his F5000 driver, Andrea de Adamich, to replace him. Adjusting quickly to the M12, de Adamich qualified sixth and finished fifth.

Michigan was a clean sweep of the first three positions for McLaren cars. Bruce (in the background with Stirling Moss) was the winner, while second-place finisher Hulme (left) and third-place finisher Gurney enjoy the champagne.

Mario Andretti and Colin Chapman check out the inner workings of the Holman Moody Ford 494-ci engine that was stuffed in the back of the ex-Shelby McLaren M6B.

McLaren's car gets a last-minute inspection before starting the Laguna Seca race.

When his Ferrari failed during the Sunday morning warm-up, fellow New Zealander, and former teammate, Chris Amon (center), was offered the third M8B. McLaren, Amon, and Hulme huddle here to determine team orders.

John Cordts' (99) McLaren M6B had several good results as an independent in 1969. Cordts had a fourth-place finish at Mosport, a fifth-place at St. Jovite, and a sixth-place at Laguna Seca.

Chris Amon (3) started at the back of the pack because he never had a chance to qualify the McLaren for the race. Amon moved quickly through the field before hitting a tire marker and pitted for a new nose section. Returning to the race, Amon was finally put out by differential failure.

Looking like rush hour on the Corkscrew, Dan Gurney's (48) McLeagle, George Eaton's (98) McLaren M12, Jo Siffert's (0) Porsche 917PA, Chuck Parsons' (10) Lola T163, and Mario Andretti's (1) McLaren M6B battle for position. Parsons finished third, Andretti finished fourth, and Siffert finished fifth.

Mario Andretti (1) and his McLaren M6B ran a strong race at Laguna Seca and finished fourth overall.

Once again, Bruce and Denny cruised an easy win.

McLaren wins his fifth race of the season at Laguna Seca.

Bruce McLaren had no luck at Riverside. He went through two engines before the race started, and suspension failure caused him to crash, unhurt, in Turn 1 during the race.

There simply was no substitute for cubic inches. Part of the secret behind McLarens success was the injected 430-ci engine.

Bruce McLaren (4) is once again hounded by that pesky Ferrari 612 (16) of Chris Amon as Dan Gurney's (48) McLeagle waits to pounce. Amon's effort with the huge 6.9-liter engine was doomed by a black flag, and Gurney, fourth overall, actually finished a race.

Mario Andretti's (1) McLaren M6B is on his way to a third overall at Riverside. Andretti leads Jackie Oliver's (22) very potent TI22 and Peter Revson's (31) Lola T163. Eventual second-place finisher Chuck Parsons (10) and his Lola T163 follows behind.

The Holman Moody McLaren M6B "429-er," driven by Mario Andretti, finished third overall at Riverside.

The AAR McLeagle was one of the most beautiful cars to compete during the 1969 season. At Riverside, the car finally overcame all of its problems and finished fourth.

Usually lucky at Riverside, Bruce McLaren had no luck there in 1969. A frightening 150-mile-per-hour crash at Turn 1 put him out of the race on lap 34.

Denny Hulme had been trying to win at Riverside for several years. Finally his luck held in 1969, and he scored his only victory there.

# CHAPTER 6

# TRAGEDY AND REBIRTH

## 1970-1971

Two weeks prior to the first Can-Am race, on June 2 to be exact, Bruce McLaren decided to do some final test laps in the new M8D built for the team to race during the 1970 Can-Am season. Tragically, after a few laps, the rear body section lifted off the car, causing it to go into a high-speed, uncontrollable spin resulting in the fatal accident that killed Bruce McLaren.

Bruce's death was not the only tragedy to beset the McLaren team before the season began. Denny Hulme seriously burned his hands during a test run in the new McLaren Indianapolis car at the Indianapolis Motor Speedway. However, after McLaren's tragic accident, nothing, including doctor's orders, could keep Hulme from being at Mosport for the first race on June 14, 1970.

A brief windfall for the team did occur, however, when Dan Gurney, who had scaled back his international appearances in favor of developing and driving Indianapolis cars and driving in the Trans Am, stepped forward to volunteer his services to the team. Unfortunately, a conflict of oil contracts forced Gurney to leave the team after the third race. The McLaren team brought in British F5000 champion Peter Gethin to finish the season. The McLaren team went on to win nine of the ten scheduled races, and Denny Hulme came away with his second championship.

The M8D, of which three were built for the 1970 season, was known as The Batmobile because of its high side fins on the rear body section. The car was of monocoque construction with the engine and

Lothar Motschenbacher's (11) McLaren M8D leads Hiroshi Kazato's (88) Lola T222 over the crest of the hill at St. Jovite in the 1971 race. Motschenbacher, a stalwart-McLaren-man, embodied the spirit of Can-Am: "We always had problems with money because we never had a major sponsor. There were a lot of things that I would have liked to do, but we could never afford to do them. In spite of those problems, racing in the Can-Am was one of the greatest experiences of my life. The times and the camaraderie that we shared then was something that I will remember for the rest of my life. It was absolutely priceless."

transmission forming part of the rear chassis. The car was powered by a 465-cid, aluminum Chevrolet engine that, when fitted with Lucas fuel injection, cranked out 670 horsepower. Like its predecessor, the M8D used a Hewland LG 500 four-speed gearbox. Longtime company sponsors Gulf Oil provided the fuel, Reynolds the engine blocks, Goodyear the tires, and Bosch the spark plugs. There was a high demand for the new customer car, and in all, 15 M8Cs were built by Trojan.

The 1971 M8F was essentially an updated version of the M8D. Gordon Coppuck improved the handling, braking, and aerodynamics by increasing the wheelbase by 3 inches, narrowing the track front and rear to accommodate wider wheels and tires, mounted larger inboard rear brakes, and improved the body shape. The car was powered by a 494-ci aluminum Chevrolet that developed a peak 740-brake horsepower at 6,400 rpm. McLaren modified the Lucas fuel injection and introduced the new Hewland LG Mk.2 four-speed unit to the car. The customer car for 1971 was called the M8E, and its most noticeable change was that it had a low wing instead of the high side fins of the M8D.

During the 1971 season, for the first time in a long time, the McLaren team would have some serious competition. This was initially provided by Jackie Stewart and the Lola T260, who won two of the first five races. Unfortunately for the fans and the series, handling trouble would plague the Lola, and its challenge fizzled as the season wore on.

Peter Revson joined Denny Hulme on the McLaren Can-Am team in 1971 and became the first American to ever win the Can-Am championship. In all, Peter won 5 of the 10 scheduled races that year with Hulme winning another three. The McLaren team came away with eight wins and their fifth consecutive Can-Am championship. The year 1971 would bring McLaren their final Can-Am championship.

> *I did it [joined the team] for Bruce, who had been a close friend of mine for many years. I really wasn't planning to run the Can-Am that year, but that team really needed help.*
> —DAN GURNEY

Dan Gurney joined the McLaren team at Mosport in 1970 under the worst possible conditions. McLaren had been killed just two weeks prior to the start of the season, and Denny Hulme's hands were very severely burned at Indianapolis when his fuel filler cap opened during practice. Here, Gurney gets fitted to the car prior to practice. Note the extra-high windscreen to accommodate Gurney's height. "I did it [joined the team] for Bruce, who had been a close friend of mine for many years. I really wasn't planning to run the Can-Am that year, but that team really needed help in the driving department, especially with Denny getting burned at Indianapolis, and I thought that I could help them. I would have liked to run the full season, but I knew that eventually I would have some serious problems regarding the Gulf oil contract." —Dan Gurney

Denny Hulme, his hands encased in gloves to protect the bandages, inspects his engine at Mosport. "I don't know how Denny managed to drive that car with the terrible pain that I know he was in. A lesser man couldn't have done it, but Denny was so focused on keeping the team together that he was able to block all of the bad things out."—Dan Gurney

*I should never have been driving at that time.*
—DENNY HULME

Denny Hulme led the Mosport race until bleeding hands and an overheating engine forced him to fade to third place. Hulme told me several years back, "I should never have been driving at that time. The doctors were extremely concerned about the possibility of infection in my hands and, if it hadn't have been for the team situation at that time, I wouldn't have been out there."

Lothar Motschenbacher drove one of the three McLaren M8Bs from the previous season in 1970. "That was the best car that I ever drove. When we first got that car, we went out to Riverside and tested it, with the high wing and the 1969 setup, and it was fantastic. I knew that I couldn't match the new car [M8D] in speed, but I always felt good if I could better the times than those the team had set the previous year with the same car."—Lothar Motschenbacher

Dan Gurney at speed. In spite of never seeing or sitting in the M8D prior to arriving at Mosport, Dan was the fastest in practice and qualifying. Note the extension piece on the rollbar that, in addition to the windscreen, was added to accommodate Gurney's height. "That Mosport race stands out as one of the better races that I drove. Denny's hands had been badly burned at Indianapolis and Jackie Oliver was driving that lightweight TI22 car, which was powered by a big-block Chevrolet 496-cid engine. Oliver's car did not handle that well, but it was very quick and Jackie was a very aggressive driver. I was running behind Denny and Jackie when Denny waved me by. I had to run my heart out to catch and stay with Oliver, who was leading at that time. Getting by Jackie was not an easy riddle to solve, and I had to really dig deep to solve that riddle. As you know, I was unfamiliar with the McLaren M8D because I had never sat in it until I got to Mosport, and I did not know just how far I could push it without getting into serious trouble. Jackie drove a great race, and when I got right up on his tail, I would lose the good air and the McLaren would start to badly understeer. I was finally able to get by, barely, on the straight and win the race."—Dan Gurney

John Cordts (57) had a new 1970 production model McLaren M8C for the season opener, but engine and transmission problems hindered his chances in the first two races. Trojan built 15 of these cars.

Although the Gulf sponsorship stickers appeared on Gurney's front fenders, the patches did not appear anywhere on his driving uniform. Here, Dan charges to his first, and McLaren's, win of the season.

Dan Gurney displays his famous smile on the Mosport victory stand. Note the small Gulf patch taped over the Castrol patch on Dan's right arm.

Dan Gurney hurdles over the door of his M8D as practice starts at St. Jovite. "I was extremely loyal to Castrol because they had been with me for a lot of years," Gurney said. "Grady Davis from Gulf didn't like my situation and wasn't about to compromise because of it. My motivation was to help Bruce's team because they needed help. The McLaren team needed some continuity and some direction at that time, and that was the primary reason that I offered to drive for them. I was not there to worry about the politics of oil company contracts. To get tangled up in that Gulf-Castrol situation was really unproductive, and it was because of that, that I left the team after the third race at Watkins Glen."

The green flag has fallen and our boy Dan (48) is already pulling out to a healthy lead over Denny Hulme's (5) McLaren M8D, Jackie Oliver's (22) TI22, Lothar Motschenbacher's (11) McLaren M8B, John Cordts' (57) McLaren M8C, and Bob Brown's (3) McLeagle. "At St. Jovite, Jackie got away with Denny and I at the start, but he got himself upside down midway through the first lap and destroyed his car," said Gurney. "I won that race, but I didn't feel any great achievement by doing it, and I think that was one of the things that helped solidify my decision to quit driving at the end of the season."

Graeme Lawrence was one of New Zealand's top F5000 drivers at the time he came over to North America to drive the "Spirit of Edmonton" McLaren M12. Unfortunately for Lawrence, the team was underfinanced, and he was never able to reach his potential in a car beset by mechanical problems. Lawrence's best finish was an eighth-place finish at Road America.

Lothar Motschenbacher was to have his finest year in the Can-Am series in 1970. Driving his favorite car, the M8B, Lothar finished second in the season championship. Note the low wing mounted on the back of the M8B. High wings were banned after the 1969 season.

> *I couldn't stay with him especially in the early races, and he was certainly fast enough to have kept the points lead even after my hands mended.*
> —DENNY HULME SPEAKING ABOUT DAN GURNEY

The courage of Denny Hulme certainly showed up during the first few Can-Am races of the 1970 season. It didn't take long for Hulme to hit his stride, and by the third race of the season he began to win again.

After the St. Jovite race, Gurney was two for two in the win category. In later years Hulme told me that if it hadn't been for the oil contract dispute, Gurney would have won the 1970 championship.

Gurney's winning streak ran out at Watkins Glen when he finished ninth after several pit stops to add water to an overheating engine. Dan left the McLaren team after this race.

British F5000 champion Peter Gethin (sitting in the car) was hired to take Gurney's place on the Can-Am team starting at Edmonton. Denny Hulme watches as Gethin acquaints himself with the unfamiliar surroundings of the M8D cockpit.

Peter Gethin takes time to sign a young admirer's program.

Denny Hulme consults with his crew about the fact that the newer car couldn't reach the lap times of the M8B the previous year.

The jockey-sized Peter Gethin looked lost in a car fitted to a much taller Dan Gurney.

Denny Hulme (5) breaks from the pole position and leads the following away from the start at Edmonton: Peter Gethin (48), Bob Brown (3) and his McLeagle, Lothar Motschenbacher's (11) McLaren M8B, George Eaton's (98) BRM P154, John Cordts' (57) McLaren M8C, and Gary Wilson's (19) Lola T163.

The teacher (5), Denny Hulme, shows the student (48), Peter Gethin, how it's done. The two McLaren drivers finished Edmonton in this order.

*Racing in the Can-Am was one of the greatest experiences of my life. The times and the camaraderie . . . [were] absolutely priceless.*—LOTHAR MOTSCHENBACHER

Denny checks his still-tender hand after the victory ceremony at Edmonton.

Another victory for Denny Hulme at Mid-Ohio later in the year.

What started out to be a walk in the park at Laguna Seca for Hulme (5) and Gethin in October 1970 turned out to be anything but. Gethin spun off the course on lap 37 and couldn't restart his car, and Denny was in for the race of his life when a rejuvenated challenger in the form of Jackie Oliver and the new TI22 Mk. II came on strong in the second half of the race.

Tony Adamowicz's (12) McLaren M12 drove a great race at Laguna Seca and finished seventh overall. Here Adamowicz leads John Cannon (15) in the Ford G7A. Cannon did not finish.

Peter Bryant had rebuilt the TI22 after the first one was destroyed at St. Jovite. This new, rebuilt car also proved that it just might become the "McLaren Slayer" that many people had hoped the first one would be. Jackie Oliver's (22) TI22 chases Denny Hulme (5) down the corkscrew, as fourth-place finisher Chris Amon (77) and his March 707 is caught in the middle. The nose-to-tail battle between Hulme and Oliver was the highlight of the season, but by the end of the race, Oliver's engine began to sputter and Hulme went on to win by 1.2 seconds.

Denny Hulme in the winner's circle at Laguna Seca. Hulme won his second Can-Am championship in 1970.

Peter Gethin blew his engine on lap 21 as his teammate Denny Hulme cruised to another win at Riverside.

Well-known and liked, American driver Peter Revson (left) joined Denny Hulme on the McLaren team in 1971.

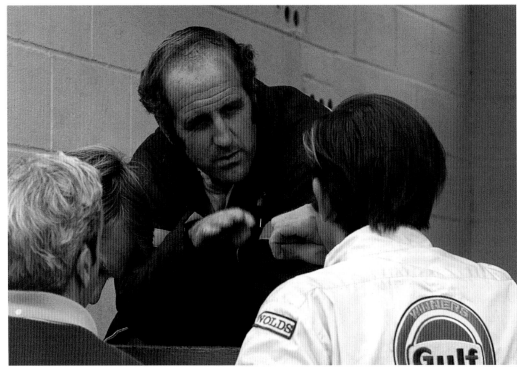

Denny Hulme (center), Peter Revson (back to camera), Tyler Alexander (barely visible at left), and Teddy Mayer (left) hold a strategy meeting before practice at St. Jovite.

Denny Hulme put his McLaren M8F on the pole at St. Jovite and took an early lead over the field. Hulme had won at Mosport, but it wasn't to be at St. Jovite. Gordon Dewar (47) and his March 707 trails Hulme.

Chuck Parsons (8) drove an independent McLaren M8D in 1971 and had a fine fourth-place finish at St. Jovite.

Some of Denny Hulme's problems at St. Jovite was illness, but the rest was the very capable challenge mounted by Jackie Stewart's (1) Lola T260. The Lola upset the apple cart and won that marque's first Can-Am race since John Surtees did it at Las Vegas in 1967.

> *Driving in the Can-Am was a great experience, and I wouldn't have traded it for the world.*—BOB BONDURANT

Bob Bondurant drove a McLaren M8E/D for the Motschenbacher team in the first four races of the 1971 season. Bondurant's best finish was a fourth at Mosport, but a disagreement at Watkins Glen prevented him from finishing the season. "The car that I drove for Lothar in 1971 was built up out of spare parts, but it was a very good car," Bondurant said. "One thing I really liked about that car was that it had plenty of horsepower. That was one thing that I really loved about the Can-Am cars, they had plenty of incredible horsepower. I had only four races in that car because Lothar and I had had a disagreement at Watkins Glen, and he fired me. My best race was my first race, and that was at Mosport. I finished fourth behind Denny, Peter, and Lothar, and I felt really good about that since I had almost no time in the car. The other three races weren't so good because we never really had the money to keep the cars going the way that they should have. Driving in the Can-Am was a great experience, and I wouldn't have traded it for the world."—Bob Bondurant

Peter Revson won his third race of the season at Road America. Note the "Go Gulf McLaren" stickers pasted on the side of the winner's trophy. Augie Pabst stands in the foreground.

Peter Revson is on the gas as he leads Denny Hulme (5) and David Hobbs' (29) TI22 Mk. II down Laguna Seca's famed corkscrew.

Denny Hulme won three races in 1971 and finished second in the year-end point standings.

Steve Matchett's (87) Porsche 908 leads three McLarens; George Drolsom's (34) McLaren M8C, Jay Hills' (81) McLaren M6B, Chuck McConnell's (33) McLaren M6B, and a Lola, Bill Cupp's (16) Lola T163, during the Laguna Seca race. Matchett was the best finisher of the bunch at 13th overall.

Vic Elford's (2) McLaren M8E/D rejoined the Can-Am series at Road Atlanta and had two top-five finishes (third at Road America and fourth at Donnybrooke) during the 1971 season.

Chuck Parsons replaced Bondurant on the Motschenbacher team and had his best finish of the year at Riverside, where he placed fifth overall.

Local southern California hero Lothar Motschenbacher had a large fan club at Riverside in October 1971.

Peter Revson had to finish sixth or better to beat out his teammate Denny Hulme for the Can-Am championship at Riverside. He finished second.

Riverside race winner Denny Hulme can be seen in the background, but all eyes are on second-place finisher Peter Revson because he has just become the first American to ever win the Can-Am Championship. Revson won five of the ten races in 1971. Hulme won three, and Stewart and his Lola won two.

# CHAPTER 7

# END OF AN ERA

## 1972 - 1974

For the 1972 Can-Am season the McLaren team announced the signing of Jackie Stewart to partner Denny Hulme in the new M20 sports car. Stewart tested the new McLaren at Silverstone but became ill prior to the start of the season, forcing him to withdraw from the team on advice of his doctors. At the last minute, McLaren recalled 1971 Can-Am champion Peter Revson from the Formula One team to which he had been promoted. Together with Hulme, the two were on hand when the season opened at Mosport in June.

The McLaren domination of the previous five years would now be seriously challenged by the new turbocharged Porsche 917/10K entered by Penske Racing and driven by Mark Donohue and George Follmer. McLaren intended to launch the M20 with a turbocharged Chevrolet engine, but it couldn't be sorted out in time. Instead, the new car appeared with the 8.1-liter, aluminum Chevrolet engine. The new car's water radiators were now mounted on either side of the monocoque chassis, instead of in the car's nose. The Gordon Coppuck–designed car also featured a full-width wing that was mounted between the front fenders in order to improve the car's downthrust when combined with the strut-mounted wing on the rear body section of the car. This combination improved traction and cornering.

For the first time, an under-the-seat fuel tank that stretched the full width of the cockpit directly behind the driver's back was used. This tank was connected to two more tanks mounted in each of the side pontoons and carried a total of 79 gallons of fuel. Record-setting test results at Silverstone by both Stewart and Hulme gave the team high hopes for the new car. Three M20s were brought to North America and 10 production M8FPs were built for customers.

Unfortunately, the McLaren effort wasn't enough to offset the huge investment made by Porsche in its Can-Am program, and the orange car's domination of the series ended with just two wins in 1972. At the

At Mosport, Denny Hulme (left), Peter Revson (center), and Tyler Alexander (right) look concerned about the turn of events during qualifying. They had a right to be concerned because Porsche had just appeared with its long-rumored turbocharged 917/10K, in the hands of Mark Donohue. The writing on the wall was definitely not in McLaren's favor.

end of the season, McLaren realized that it couldn't compete with the Porsche juggernaut and withdrew from the series. Scoring 43 victories, including 19 consecutive race wins between 1968 and 1970, the McLaren team set records that would never be approached by another team. Without McLaren, the Can-Am series could never be the same.

By 1973, it was obvious to teams and fans alike that the Can-Am series was in serious trouble. Porsche and UOP Shadow were the only factory efforts that year and the number of quality competitors took a drastic reversal from previous years. There were no new McLarens produced for the 1973 season. The only McLarens in competition that year were ex-team cars and older customer cars. For the first time since 1966, the McLaren name did not rise to the top of the winner's rostrum.

Only five Can-Am races contested in 1974. Ironically, an ex-team M20 won the final race of the Can-Am series.

The legacy that McLaren created in the Can-Am between 1967 and 1972 is still talked about 28 years after it ended. Although the McLaren domination of the series was hotly debated at the time, it only came about through a well-conceived and well-executed plan of attack. McLaren depended on the income derived from professional sports car racing to keep the company's doors open. At that time, the Can-Am series paid better than Formula One, and, with McLaren's involvement in running Indianapolis cars, the company was stretched to the maximum.

The money won in the Can-Am series was well used to improve the company, and when the series quit being worth the investment, McLaren pulled out. After McLaren's withdrawal, the series barely survived for another season and a half before vanishing into history.

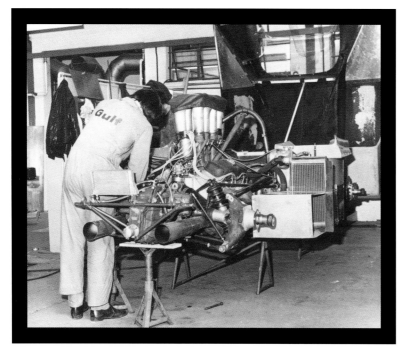

The 1972 McLaren M20 receives final touches at the Colinbrook factory before being taken to Goodwood for testing. Note the side-mounted water radiators being used for the first time on the M20.

A rare photograph of Jackie Stewart testing a McLaren M20 at Goodwood in the spring of 1972. Stewart was signed to a team with Denny Hulme for the 1972 Can-Am season but was sidelined by an ulcer before the season began. Peter Revson, who was promoted to the F1 team, was recalled to partner with Hulme.

By the time the Can-Am moved to Road Atlanta for the second race of the year, George Follmer had replaced Mark Donohue in the number 6 car due to a serious testing accident that injured Donohue's knee and destroyed one of the Porsches. When the race started, Denny (5) did his best to stay with Follmer, but on lap 4 Hulme became airborne and flipped the M20, leaving Follmer to win. Engine problems kept Revson from finishing.

The two McLarens leading the Porsche 917/10K was a sight that became extremely rare as the 1972 season progressed. At Watkins Glen, the old days returned, briefly, as the cars of Hulme (5) and Revson (5) lead George Follmer (6) early in the race.

Peter Revson (4) leads Denny Hulme (5) and many others at Watkins Glen. Revson finished second at Watkins Glen, but the defending champion had no wins during the 1972 Can-Am season.

Denny Hulme leads Charlie Kemp's (23) Lola T222 at Watkins Glen. Hulme won this race, the last Can-Am win for a McLaren team car in the series.

The first and only sweep of the top two finishing positions by the McLaren team occurred at Watkins Glen. Peter Revson (left) congratulates Denny Hulme (right) on his 22nd, and last, Can-Am win.

Denny Hulme at Watkins Glen in July 1972.

Peter Revson is on the gas at Watkins Glen in July 1972.

François Cevert (22) driving Gregg Young's McLaren M8F won the Donnybrooke race by being in the right place at the right time. The two factory McLarens blew their engines, Mark Donohue blew a tire, and George Follmer ran out of gas.

François Cevert at Laguna Seca. Cevert had one win and three other top-five finishes in 1972. He finished fifth in the final point standings.

Peter Revson qualified third behind the two Porsches at Laguna Seca. Revson leads Sam Posey's (20) Porsche 917PA but had gearbox failure on the 52nd lap and was classified 19th, even though he did not finish.

Denny Hulme qualified fifth at Laguna Seca but blew his engine on the 16th lap. Hulme leads two other competitors very early in the race.

François Cevert (22) was the star of the show at Laguna Seca. After starting last in the field due to not being able to qualify, Cevert charged through the 32-man field to finish third overall.

The McLaren team prepares for its final race at Riverside.

Peter Revson (foreground) talks to Tyler Alexander while he awaits new rubber, and Denny Hulme (background) sits through an engine check as the McLaren team prepares for practice at Riverside.

After qualifying second on the grid, Denny Hulme certainly has something to smile about with the now-retired Dan Gurney (right). Hulme had used a one-of-a-kind 565-ci, 800-brake horsepower Chevrolet engine to qualify the M20, but that engine was only good for a few laps and soon had to be replaced with the normal, more reliable 8.1-liter version.

Denny Hulme seems to be intently watching the Porsche's track performance. Could he know something that no one else, including teammate Peter Revson, knows?

Running in second position early in the race, Denny Hulme (5) leads Mark Donohue (6) and his Porsche 917/10K and Peter Revson (4) through Riverside's famed Turn 7.

The two McLaren team M20s driven by Denny Hulme (5) and Peter Revson (4) are seen running together for the last time at Riverside. Hulme lost his engine on lap 45 and was classified 19th overall. Peter Revson finished 2nd overall behind Follmer but ahead of Donohue. After the Riverside race, the McLaren team pulled the plug on its Can-Am program.

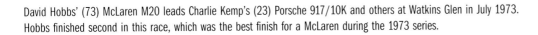

David Hobbs' (73) McLaren M20 leads Charlie Kemp's (23) Porsche 917/10K and others at Watkins Glen in July 1973. Hobbs finished second in this race, which was the best finish for a McLaren during the 1973 series.

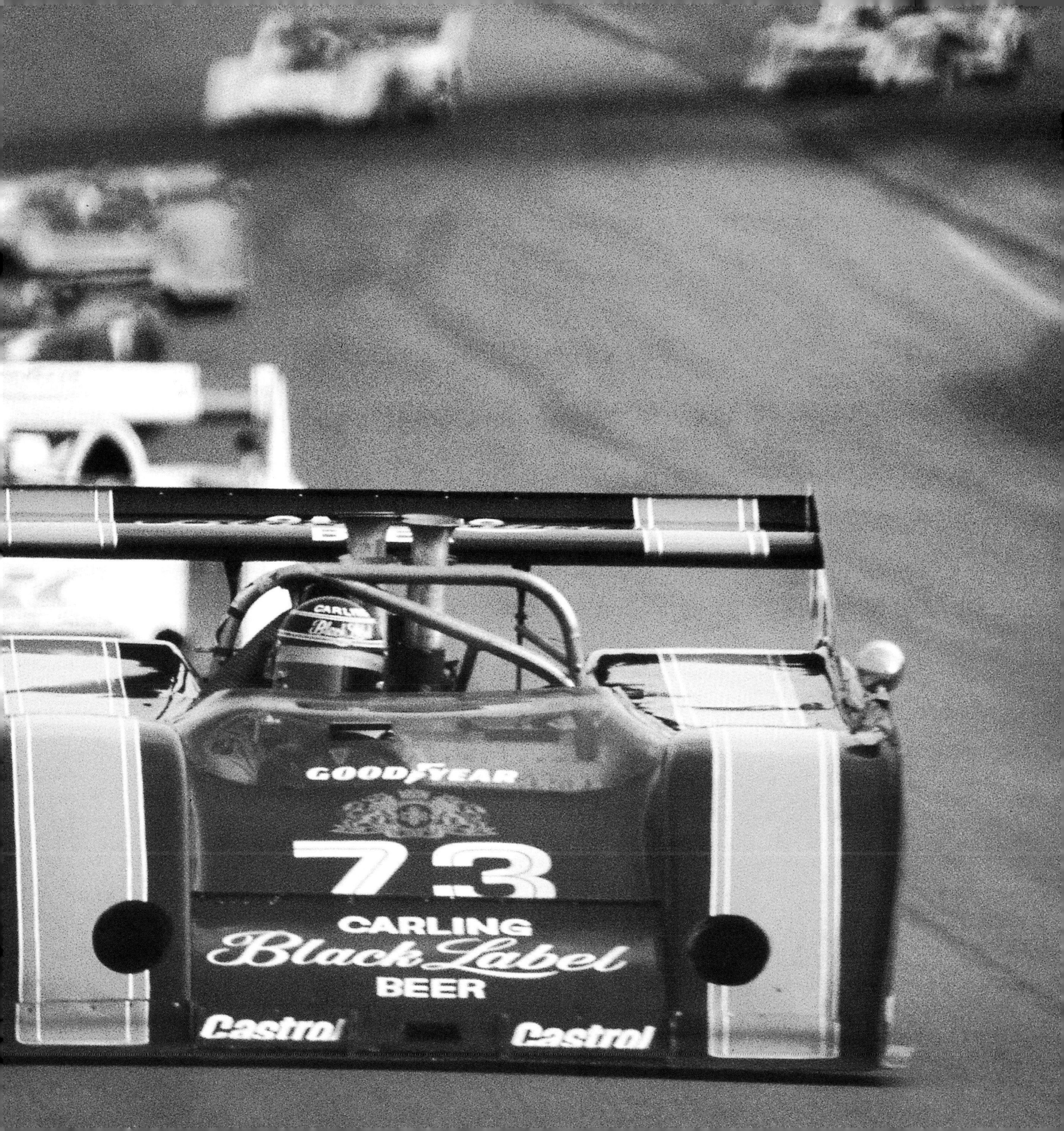
GOODYEAR
73
CARLING
Black Label
BEER
Castrol
Castrol

Bob Brown's (97) McLaren M8F leads Scooter Patrick's (8) McLaren M8F, Hans Wiedner's (4) Porsche 917/10K, Bob Nagel's (17) Lola T260, and Danny Hopkins' (98) McLaren M8F at Watkins Glen. Brown didn't finish, but Patrick finished 10th and Hopkins finished 19th.

John Cannon's (98) McLaren M8F accelerates out of Laguna Seca's Turn 9. Cannon qualified eighth but crashed on the third lap.

Scooter Patrick's (8) McLaren M8F, Hurley Haywood's (59) Porsche 917/10K, and Milt Minter's (33) Alfa Romeo T33/3 are running close through the corkscrew during the October 1973 Laguna Seca Can-Am.

Steve Durst's (11) McLaren M8F leads Bob Nagel's (17) Lola T260 and Jackie Oliver's (101) UOP Shadow out of Turn 9 at Laguna Seca. Durst had brake problems and retired on lap 45. It is interesting to note that 1973 was the first year since 1966 that a McLaren did not win a Can-Am race.

*Following pages:* How fitting it was that a McLaren won the final race that was run in the original Can-Am series. Scooter Patrick (8) McLaren M20 won the Road American Can-Am on August 25, 1974—the day the Can-Am died.

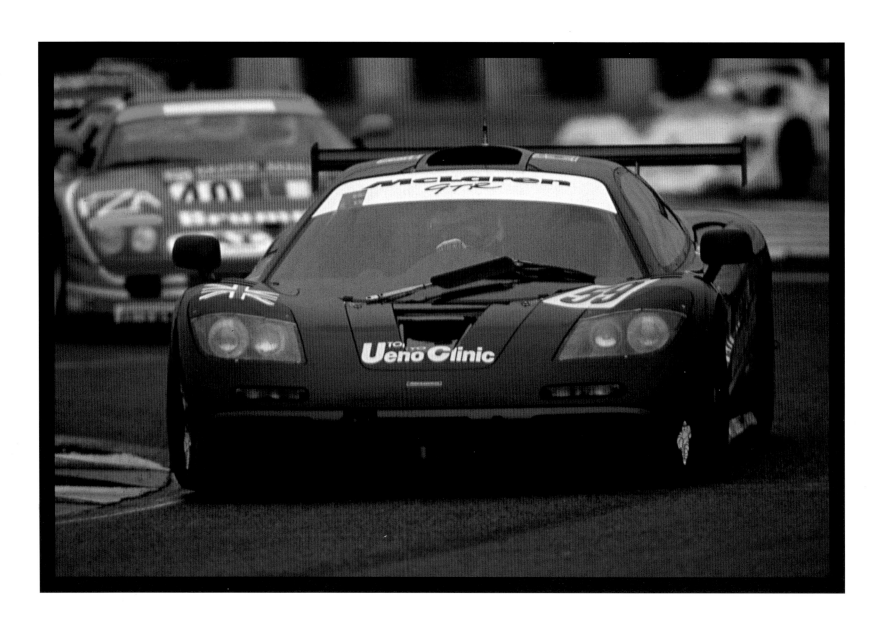

# FULL CIRCLE

## THE McLAREN F1GTR

B y 1990, the legendary McLaren sports cars experienced a rebirth. Gordon Murray, who had built himself a world-famous reputation as one of the most innovative Formula One designers of his time, felt he had other worlds to conquer. Murray dreamed of building the world's most exotic road car, and in January 1990 a three-year program was launched by McLaren Cars Ltd. to do just that. The first car was finished in late 1993, confirming Murray's quest for excellence with its unbelievable performance.

Unlike the McLaren program of years earlier, a racing version of the F1 was not in the plans this time, and it wasn't even considered until customers began to demand one for the 1995 GT racing season.

Finally the McLaren F1GTR made its racing debut in the 1995 BRP Karcher Global Endurance GT Series and won 10 of the 12 that year, reviving a McLaren tradition of racing (and winning) in sports cars. The GTR made its debut at Le Mans in June 1995 and won an unprecedented overall victory the first time out. McLaren won the series championship in 1995 and 1996. In 1997, McLaren was in the hunt for the championship but was beaten out by Mercedes in the final race of the year at Laguna Seca in 1997. By the end of 1997, McLaren completed its allocation of 100 road cars, and the FIA GT series began to fall apart. Once again, in an uncanny repeat of sports car history, it was time for McLaren to move on. The McLaren sports car legend had come full circle.

*Above:* The winners of the 1995 Le Mans 24-Hour Race—Masanori Sekiya, J. J. Lehto, and Yannick Damas—wave to the huge crowd from the winner's rostrum.

*Left:* The winning McLaren at the 1995 Le Mans 24-Hour Race. How many other marques won their first time out (besides Ferrari in 1949) with a car that was less than six months old?

Susan Claudius is about to be fitted for the car of her dreams. This mockup is used to fit the customer to his, or her, F1 cockpit.

Gordon Murray poses with the prototype McLaren F1 during the first press day preview in the spring of 1992.

An F1 nears completion at McLaren Cars Ltd. The carbon-fiber and aluminum monocoque chassis is powered by a V-12 DOHC BMW engine and reaches a top speed of 250 miles per hour.

The BMW V-12 DOHC engine develops more than 600-brake horsepower from its 6.0-liter capacity.

Customer cars ready for testing and delivery. Barely visible in the background is the first Gulf McLaren F1GTR. These shop photos were taken in March 1995.

The Gulf McLarens undergo prerace preparation prior to the Laguna Seca championship round in October 1997.

The BMW Motorsport GTR almost pulled off a third straight championship for McLaren, but they were beaten out by Mercedes in the final round at Laguna Seca in October 1997. McLaren withdrew from the series following the last race of the 1997 season, ending another period of McLaren sports racing cars.

# INDEX

BRUCE McLAREN
1937-1970